IMAGES
of America

TRADITIONAL
COUNTRY &
WESTERN MUSIC

ROSE LEE MAPHIS. When in Nashville several years ago, my wife, Susan; Rose Lee Maphis; Debby Delmore; and I attended a Marty Stuart performance at the Franklin Theatre in Franklin, Tennessee. Marty asked Rose on stage to sing "Dim Lights, Thick Smoke (And Loud Loud Music)," the country music standard she wrote with her late husband, Joe. Marty endearingly referred to Rose Lee as "country music royalty." After the concert, fans followed us down the street so they could talk to our gracious friend. Rose is a living legend and a wonderful person. She is loved and admired by her children, Lorrie and Jody, as well as those who know her. Rose Lee Schetrompf was born on a farm near Baltimore, Maryland, on December 29, 1922. Rose began singing on radio when she was 15 years old. My oldest photograph of her dates from a late-1940s *Old Dominion Barn Dance* picture album. Therefore, I called Rose Lee and asked for an older picture to include in this book. A few weeks later, an envelope arrived in the mail that contained a photograph of Rose at the age of 94. I failed to adequately communicate my request for an image of her when she was younger, but Rose Lee accurately responded by sending an "older" picture. (Courtesy of Rose Lee Maphis.)

ON THE COVER: ROY AND THE RICHMOND PIONEERS. This wonderful image captures an innocent era of country and western music in America, including the elements of a Conestoga wagon, Gibson guitar, and a junkyard dog. (Courtesy of Jack Tenschert of Reading, Pennsylvania.)

IMAGES
of America

TRADITIONAL COUNTRY & WESTERN MUSIC

Karl Anderson

ARCADIA
PUBLISHING

Published by Arcadia Publishing
Charleston, South Carolina

Printed in the United States of America

Library of Congress Control Number: 2020934451

For all general information, please contact Arcadia Publishing:
Telephone 843-853-2070
Fax 843-853-0044
E-mail sales@arcadiapublishing.com
For customer service and orders:
Toll-Free 1-888-313-2665

Visit us on the Internet at www.arcadiapublishing.com

Rose Lee was endowed with many gifts and talents. As a young girl, she made the conscious decision to be a happy and grateful person. Rose is a woman of religious faith who wears a smile and counts her blessings. This book is dedicated to our dear friend Rose Lee Maphis.

CONTENTS

ACKNOWLEDGMENTS

The photographs and memorabilia included in this book are primarily from my personal collection. However, several photographs were provided through the generous contributions of Jonathan Causey (the Sullivan Family); Larry Collins and Christy Hall Carnall (the Collins Kids); Debbie Delmore (the Delmore Brothers); Rose Lee Maphis; the Ohio County Public Library Archives in Wheeling, West Virginia (the Blue Mountain Boys); Shari Penny (Hank Penny); Gavin Wissen and the West Virginia Music Hall of Fame (Molly O'Day); and Jason Wilburn (the Wilburn Children).

A special thanks to family members, including my daughter Karla Anderson, who accepted the challenge of photography involving items that are framed and mounted under glass as well as editing my text. Also thanks to my daughter Kristina Anderson for reviewing my photograph selection and wife Susan for attempting to tolerate my compulsive behavior, ever-present laptop computer on our dining room table, and photographs scattered throughout our home.

INTRODUCTION

As a young boy, our family lived in the Allegheny Mountains of Western Pennsylvania. Traditional forms of country and western music were popular in many homes and taverns. I remember the desire to rush home so that I could listen to the Blue Mountain Boys on the radio. The group broadcast daily on WWVA, a 50,000-watt station in Wheeling, West Virginia. By today's standards, Toby Stroud and his band played bluegrass music. During those years, they were known as folk or hillbilly performers.

On Saturday nights, I would sometimes tune into the *Wheeling Jamboree*. However, it was difficult to understand the announcer or song lyrics. "Hillbilly" was a foreign language. The 1950s were wonderful years. Ike was president, and America was the leader of the free world. Baseball, Boy Scouts, and Sunday school were enjoyable rituals in my life. Folk and hillbilly music was icing on the cake.

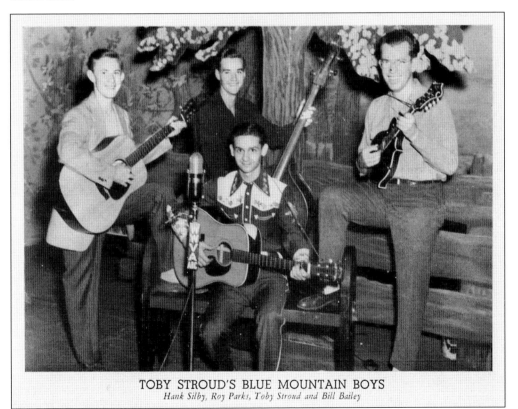

TOBY STROUD'S BLUE MOUNTAIN BOYS
Hank Silby, Roy Parks, Toby Stroud and Bill Bailey

TOBY STROUD'S BLUE MOUNTAIN BOYS. This rare photograph is of the Blue Mountain Boys in Wheeling, West Virginia, in 1946. (Courtesy of the Ohio County Public Library Archives.)

Economic hard times arrived in small-town America during the early 1960s. Our family left Pennsylvania to pursue the jobs and opportunities of Southern California, and my young life was turned upside down. Fortunately, my uncle Hugo Blymiller lived in nearby Santa Monica. His passion for the guitar and country music soon became mine.

During the 1960s, country music television programs aired every day in Los Angeles, California. Cal Worthington (a large LA auto dealer who would appear on TV advertisements riding an elephant or cuddling with a tiger) sponsored *Cal's Corral* and *Country Music Time*; both were broadcast from the Huntington Park Ballroom. In addition, there were a half-dozen country music radio stations, as well as a large number of coffee houses, clubs, and other venues that featured live country and folk music.

The purpose of this book is to acquaint you with traditional country and western music with stories and trivia about early legends, unsung heroes, and local entertainers who captured the American heart and spirit from the late 1920s through the 1960s. This music genre originated with folk music from European immigrants who settled our vast country. Cowboy music surged in popularity as a result of movie stars such as Gene Autry and Roy Rogers. After World War II, dance halls and honky-tonk bars showcased performers who wore dazzling Nudie suits while playing fiddles and steel guitars. This exciting era is gone, but there is still the memory and sound of great American music.

Hopefully, this book contributes to your enjoyment and understanding of music that has become a unique part of American culture. There are numerous Internet and cable sources where you can access and enjoy vintage country music artists performing on barn dance programs or listen to scratchy 78-rpm records.

Hugo Blymiller. This c. 1948 photograph includes Hugo "Slim" Blymiller (left). He was an amazing guitar player as well as my uncle, guitar instructor, and music mentor. Hugo introduced me to the records of Jimmie Rodgers, the Delmore Brothers, Merle Travis, and Chet Atkins.

One

Vintage Images of Legendary Country Music Artists

Carson Robison and the Buckaroos. Carson Robison (center) was a legendary performer and songwriter who was nearly forgotten by the 1960s. However, Tex Ritter's recording of "Hillbilly Heaven" reminded listeners that Robison would join Jimmie Rodgers and other country music greats would be "Rounded Up in Glory" (another Tex Ritter classic record). Carson Jay Robison (1890–1957) was born in Oswego, Kansas. In 1924, he signed a recording contract with the Victor Talking Machine Company. Robison collaborated with Vernon Dalhart, another country music pioneer. He accompanied Dalhart on the "Wreck of the Old 97" and "The Prisoner's Song" (1924), widely considered the first country music record to sell a million copies.

THE NEW CARSON ROBISON SONG ALBUM. In 1931, Robison formed the Buckaroos. The group included John and Bill Mitchell, Frank Novak, and Pearl Pickens. He was one of the first country acts to tour Great Britain and Ireland (1932, 1936, and 1939). Perhaps his most memorable recording was "Life Gets Tee Gus Don't It" (1948). Carson Robison was one of the first professional country music songwriters. His compositions included "Turkey in the Straw," "Carry Me Back to the Lone Prairie," "Little Green Valley," and "Open Up Them Pearly Gates." He was elected to the Nashville Songwriters Hall of Fame (1971) and the Western Music Hall of Fame Association (2001). The song album pictured was published in 1932 by Southern Music Publishing Company, Inc.

10

Alton & Rabon
Delmore

THE DELMORE BROTHERS. The Delmore Brothers were iconic country music performers, recording artists, and songwriters. They were one of the great brother acts and early stars of the *Grand Ole Opry* (1933–1939) before gaining renewed prominence as performers on WLW in Cincinnati, Ohio. In 1943, Alton Delmore (left) and Ramon Delmore (right) formed a legendary gospel quartet known as the Brown's Ferry Four. The group also included Merle Travis, Grandpa Jones, and Red Foley. Along with the harmonica genius of Wayne Raney, the Delmore Brothers composed and recorded some of their most famous songs during the late 1940s—"Hillbilly Boogie," "Freight Train Boogie," and "Blues Stay Away from Me." The group disbanded in 1952. Soon after, Rabon died of lung cancer. Alton retired in Huntsville, Alabama, where he made his living from song royalties and giving guitar lessons. He also wrote a well-acclaimed but unfinished autobiography, *Truth Is Stranger than Publicity.* (Courtesy of Debby Delmore.)

DELMORE BROTHERS POSTER. The group played in concert at the Cotton Bowl Theatre in Lepanto, Arkansas, on Wednesday, September 4, 1946, promoted by this rare boxing-style poster. Among numerous lifetime achievements and awards, the Delmore Brothers were inducted into the Alabama Music Hall of Fame (1989), Independent Country Music Association–Germany (2000), and Country Music Hall of Fame (2001). Their 1949 recording of "Blues Stay Away from Me" was inducted into the Grammy Hall of Fame.

STEWART HAMBLEN AND HIS GANG. This c. 1934 Star Outfitting Company advertisement includes, from left to right, (first row) Norman Leroy Hedges, Stuart Hamblen, and George Clinton "Shug" Fisher Jr.; (second row) Vince "Bullet" Engle, Joe ?, Dave Ashenfelder, Herman the Hermit, Frank Liddell, and Bob Hatfield. Note that this photograph incorrectly identifies Shug Fisher as "Sug" and Stuart Hamblen as "Stewart." Carl Stuart Hamblen (1908–1989) enjoyed a successful career as a singer, radio personality, cowboy movie actor, and songwriter. Stuart's compositions included "Texas Plains," "Remember Me (I'm the One Who Loves You)," and "I Won't Go Huntin' with You Jake (But I'll Go Chasin' Women)," as well as gospel classics such as "This Ole House" and "It Is No Secret (What God Can Do)." In 1926, Hamblen appeared on WBAP and WFAA in Dallas–Fort Worth, Texas, as radio's first singing cowboy. From 1931 to 1952, Stuart had the number-one radio show on the West Coast. In 1934, he became the first artist signed by Decca Records. Stuart was a talented horse rider and leading trainer at Santa Anita Race Track. In 1947, he became the first person to fly a horse (El Lobo, a Santa Anita Handicap winner) from Los Angeles to Burlingame, California, for a race. He appeared in numerous films with John Wayne, Gene Autry, and Roy Rogers. Stuart earned a reputation as a heavy drinker, gambler, and street brawler. In 1949, he experienced religious conversion at a Billy Graham crusade in Los Angeles. He vowed to quit gambling and take up a sober lifestyle. As a result of his stand against alcohol, Stuart's career in radio came to an abrupt end. He ran for president on the Prohibition Party ticket against Dwight D. Eisenhower in 1952 and received about 70,000 votes. In 1971, Stuart returned to the radio airwaves with *Cowboy Church of the Air.* Stuart Hamblen was inducted into the Nashville Songwriters Hall of Fame (1970), received the Academy of Country Music Pioneer Award (1971), was inducted into the Gospel Music Hall of Fame (1994), Western Music Hall of Fame (1999), Texas Country Music Hall of Fame (2001), and Southern Gospel Music Association Hall of Fame (2012).

Patsy Montana. Ruby Rose Blevins (1908–1996) was born in Beaudry, Arkansas. In 1929, she moved to California to study violin at the University of the West (later renamed the University of California–Los Angeles). Blevins won a talent contest and soon became a regular performer on Stuart Hamblen's radio program. Hamblen gave her the name "Patsy Montana" when he introduced her as the niece of Monty Montana, a guest star on his show. Patsy moved to Chicago to perform at the 1933 World's Fair. She appeared with the Prairie Ramblers as regular performers on the WLS *National Barn Dance*. In 1935, the group recorded "I Want to Be a Cowboy's Sweetheart." She became the first female country music artist to sell a million records. Patsy adapted the song from Stuart Hamblen's signature composition "Texas Plains." She appeared in several movies, including *Colorado Sunset* with Gene Autry. Shortly after her death, Patsy was inducted into the Country Music Hall of Fame (1996).

VOGUE RECORD OF "WHEN I GETS TO WHERE I'M GOIN'." Vogue picture records were manufactured by Sav-Way Industries of Detroit, Michigan, and initially released in May 1946. Production ceased in April 1947 after release of approximately 74 different 10-inch picture records. The records were initially popular because of their colorful artwork. According to the Association of Vogue Picture Record Collectors, the records were of a very high quality with little surface noise. The records were manufactured using a complex process where a central core aluminum disc was sandwiched between paper illustrations and vinyl.

TEX ATCHISON. This photograph shows Tex Atchison (fiddle), Skeeter Shepherd (guitar), and Smokey Armstrong (bass) in fancy Western attire. Shelby David "Tex" Atchison (1904–1982) was born in Rosine, Kentucky. Country music historian Charles K. Wolfe called him "arguably the best left handed fiddle player in the history of country music." Tex was born on the farm next to Bill Monroe. They attended school together, but their musical paths took different directions. When Atchison was 14 years old, he became a member of Faught's Entertainers, which included Arnold Schultz, the legendary black guitar player. The group combined country and Dixieland music. Tex worked in coal mines during the day and played fiddle, saxophone, and clarinet at night. In 1932, Atchison left his coal mine employment and joined Chick Hurt and Salty Holmes to form a group called the Kentucky Ramblers, later known as the Prairie Ramblers. In 1933, the group joined the WLS *National Barn Dance*. During the 1940s, Tex moved to Hollywood and became a member of Foy Willing and the Riders of the Purple Sage. He appeared in more than 30 Charles Starrett films with Jimmy Wakely and Johnny Bond. He was also an equestrian stunt rider in the movies and wrote more than 300 songs. Atchison's fiddle can be heard on many recordings of Tex Ritter, Tennessee Ernie Ford, and Merle Travis.

HANK PENNY. This c. 1938 photograph of Hank Penny's band includes, from left to right, Louis Dumont (banjo), Sheldon Bennett (fiddle), Noel "Peewee" Boggs (steel guitar), Carl Stewart (bass), Boudleaux Bryant (fiddle), and Hank Penny (guitar). Herbert Clayton "Hank" Penny (1918–1992) was born in Birmingham, Alabama. He was a Western swing bandleader and a comedian. Hank formed the Radio Cowboys in the 1930s and appeared on the WLW *Midwest Hayride* during the mid-1940s. In the late 1940s, Hank moved to Southern California and appeared as "That Plain Ol' Country Boy" on Spade Cooley's telephone show. He became a regular in Forman Phillips's barn dance at the Venice Pier. By 1954, Hank began a seven-year engagement at the Golden Nugget in Las Vegas. He continued as an active performer through the 1980s. Boudleaux Bryant later became a songwriter who composed "Rocky Top," "All I Have to Do Is Dream," and other hits. (Courtesy of Shari Penny.)

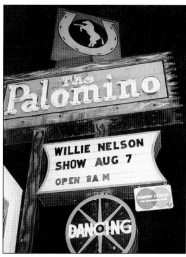

THE PALOMINO CLUB. In 1949, Armand Gautier and Hank opened the famous Palomino Club in North Hollywood, California. The Palomino was the number-one country music night club in the Los Angeles area until it closed in 1995. (Courtesy of Shari Penny.)

17

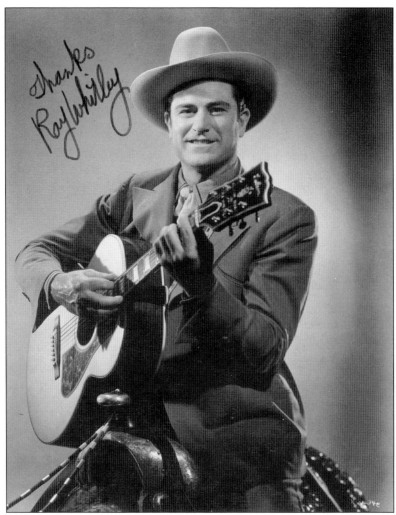

RAY WHITLEY. Raymond Otis "Ray" Whitley (1901–1979) was born in Atlanta, Georgia. In 1930, he moved to New York City, where he was employed as a steel worker on the construction of the Empire State Building and the George Washington Bridge. While in New York, Ray auditioned at a local radio station as a pop singer and accompanied himself on the guitar. Soon thereafter, he formed the Range Ramblers and broadcast on WMCA in New York. He then traveled with Colonel Johnson's World Championship Rodeo Organization and renamed his band the Six Bar Cowboys. Ray was an expert with a bullwhip and could remove a cigarette from someone's lips with a single stroke. In 1937, Ray Whitley consulted with Gibson on the design and production of the SJ-200, which became an iconic American guitar. The first Gibson SJ-200 built for Whitley is displayed at the Country Music Hall of Fame. In 1938, Ray signed a contract with RKO Pictures, and he appeared in 59 movies, including *Giant*, which starred Elizabeth Taylor, Rock Hudson, and James Dean. Whitley was an accomplished songwriter. In 1938, he was awakened by an early morning call from RKO Studios. They wanted a new Western song for a motion picture. Whitley remarked to his wife, "Well, it looks like I'm back in the saddle again." His wife recognized a good song title, and Ray wrote the first verse of "Back in the Saddle," a song that would ensure his legacy as a singing cowboy. According to Wes Tuttle, the song was sold to Gene Autry for $50. Ray was inducted into the Atlanta Country Music Hall of Fame (1995), Nashville Songwriters Hall of Fame (1981), and Western Music Association Hall of Fame (1996).

THE BLUE SKY BOYS

Bill Bolick   Earl Bolick   Curly Parker

THE BLUE SKY BOYS. This photograph of the Blue Sky Boys includes Earl Bolick (guitar), Bill Bolick (mandolin), and Sam "Curly" Parker (fiddle). They were known for close harmony and became one of the most popular brother acts in country music history. Their best-selling recordings include "Sunny Side of Life" and "Are You From Dixie." They recorded songs of unrequited love, poverty, death and despair, the ravages of war, murder, and spending life in prison (music to slit your wrists by). However, their gospel selections offered a message of hope and redemption. The Blue Sky Boys were the soul of traditional country music. William A. "Bill" Bolick (1917–2008) and Earl Alfred Bolick (1919–1998) were born in Hickory, North Carolina. In 1935, Bill and Earl made their radio debut on WWNC in Asheville, North Carolina. Six months later, they moved to WGST in Atlanta, Georgia, and became known as the Blue Ridge Hillbillies. The boys signed a recording contract with RCA Records and were labeled the "new hillbilly kings." They changed their name to the Blue Sky Boys, since the name of their group was being used by a former member. In 1936, they made their first recording, their signature song "Sunny Side of Life." The Blue Sky Boys recorded nearly 125 songs for RCA and Bluebird Records. Many prewar recordings of the Blue Sky Boys were reissued by RCA during the early 1960s.

BLUE SKY BOYS POSTER. From 1941 to 1946, the group was disbanded while the brothers served in the US Army. After World War II, the Blue Sky Boys resumed their radio and recording career. They enjoyed a number of hit records, including "Kentucky." They stopped recording for a while when RCA asked them to use electric guitar and sing newer songs. Bill and Earl retired in 1951 because of personal disagreements and the change in popularity from hillbilly to honky-tonk music. During the early 1960s, Starday Records released an album of radio transcriptions by the Blue Sky Boys. The brothers reunited and recorded two albums for Starday. During a trip to California, they appeared at the UCLA Folk Festival and recorded an album for Capitol Records. They continued to perform at folk revival and bluegrass festivals for several years. The Blue Sky Boys were inducted into the Atlanta Country Music Hall of Fame (1985). In 2018, a book by Dick Spottswood, *The Blue Sky Boys*, was released by the University Press of Mississippi. This is a rare boxing-style poster of a Blue Sky Boys performance in 1949.

AL DEXTER. Clarence Albert Poindexter (1905–1984), known as Al Dexter, was born in Jacksonville, Texas. Al was a singer and songwriter who gained fame for his composition and recording of "Pistol Packin' Mama." During 1943–1944, the song was number one on the pop hit parade for eight consecutive weeks and sold a reported three million copies. Al Dexter is considered a pioneer of honky-tonk music. His 1936 composition and recording of "Honky Tonk Blues" is said to be first time the word was used in a country music song. Other compositions included "Guitar Polka," "Rosalita," and "Too Late to Worry, Too Blue to Cry." He was inducted into the Nashville Songwriters Hall of Fame (1971).

ELTON BRITT. James Elton Baker, later known as Elton Britt (1913–1972) was born near Marshall, Arkansas. As a baby, he was very sickly and frail. His parents did not expect their boy to live. As a result, they did not name him until he was more than a year old. The Bakers were a musical family, and Elton started playing guitar at the age of 10. Elton learned the records of Jimmie Rodgers and how to yodel. His first big break came in 1930, when he became a member of the Beverly Hill Billies. The group played nearly every day on KMPC-AM in Los Angeles. A station employee commented that "James Baker" did not resonate like the name of a hillbilly singer and suggested a change to Elton Britt. In 1934, Britt recorded "Chime Bells," a yodeling classic that brought attention to his billing as the "World's Highest Yodeler." In 1942, he recorded "There's a Star-Spangled Banner Waving Somewhere." The record sold more than four million copies and was symbolic of American patriotism during World War II. He received an invitation to entertain President Roosevelt at the White House. Elton recorded more than 50 albums with RCA before moving to ABC Paramount in 1957. Eight years later, he recorded the "Jimmie Rodgers Blues," which was number 26 on the charts. In the meantime, Britt retired several times, mined uranium, and sought the Democratic nomination for president in 1960. He was inducted into the Yodeling Hall of Fame (date unknown) and received a star on the Hollywood Walk of Fame in 1960.

FLOYD TILLMAN. Floyd Tillman (1914–2003) was born in Ryan, Oklahoma. As a young man, Tillman moved to San Antonio, Texas, where he began his career as a lead guitar player for Adolph Hofner, a Western swing bandleader. He also worked with Ted Daffan (the bandleader who composed "Truck Drive Blues" and "Born to Lose") and Moon Mullican ("King of the Hillbilly Piano Players"). However, Floyd's real talent was writing songs that helped define Western swing and honky-tonk music. Tillman's first hit was "It Makes No Difference Now," a song he sold to Jimmie Davis for $300. Other successes included "Drivin' Nails in My Coffin," "Slippin' Around" and "I Love You So Much It Hurts Me." Tillman was elected to the Nashville Songwriters Hall of Fame (1970), Country Music Hall of Fame (1984), and America's Old Time Country Music Hall of Fame (2003).

T. TEXAS TYLER. David Luke Myrick (1916–1972), whose stage name was "T. Texas Tyler," was born in Mena, Arkansas. He was known as "The Man with a Million Friends." The most memorable recordings of T. Texas Tyler and the Oklahoma Melody Boys included "Remember Me (When the Candle Lights Are Gleaming)" (1945), his composition "Deck of Cards" (1948), and "Dad Gave My Dog Away" (1948). T. Texas Tyler struggled with drugs and alcohol. In 1958, he experienced religious conversion at a Foursquare Gospel church in Long Beach, California. He became an ordained minister for the Assembly of God Church and preached throughout the United States and Canada. Following the death of his wife in 1968, he remarried and moved to Springfield, Missouri, where he became a minister to a local congregation.

Molly O'Day. This is a rare photograph of Molly O'Day and her brother "Skeets" Williamson. Lois LaVerne Williamson (1923–1987), later known as Molly O'Day, was born on a farm in McVeigh, Kentucky. Her father was a coal miner. Although neither parent played music, Lois performed with her two brothers, Cecil "Skeets" (fiddle) and Joe "Duke" Williamson (banjo). In 1939, Skeets joined Ervin Staggs and His Radio Ramblers on WCHS in Charleston, West Virginia. That same year, Lois also joined the Radio Ramblers as "Mountain Fern." In 1940, she and her brothers joined John Bailes and the Happy Valley Boys. However, the group was unable to earn a living and disbanded later that same year. Around 1941, Lois joined Lynn Davis and the Forty-Niners. A few months later, Lynn and Lois were married, and Lois adopted her stage name. They performed at venues throughout the South, including a tour with Hank Williams. In 1945, Lynn changed the band's name to the Cumberland Mountain Folks. In 1946, Fred Rose heard Molly sing "Tramp on the Street," a song she had learned from Hank Williams. Rose arranged for Molly to sign a recording contract with Columbia Records. From 1946 to 1951, she recorded for Columbia with the Cumberland Mountain Folks, with Lynn Davis (banjo), Skeets Williamson (fiddle), George "Speedy" Krise (dobro), and Mac Wiseman (bass). Molly had serious concerns about her career as an entertainer. She retired from music to become a minister for the Church of God. Molly began preaching and performing gospel music throughout the coal-mining communities of West Virginia. In 1974, Lynn and Molly started a gospel music program on a Christian radio station in Huntington, West Virginia. Molly was one of the great female singers of traditional country music. She was also a talented banjo player. Earl Scruggs once said that he lost a banjo contest to her. Molly O'Day was inducted into the West Virginia Music Hall of Fame (2015). (Courtesy of the West Virginia Music Hall of Fame.)

MAC WISEMAN

Dot Records

MAC WISEMAN. Malcolm Bell "Mac" Wiseman (1925–2019) was born near Crimora, Virginia. He was stricken with polio at the age of six with resulting disabilities that kept him from field labor and physical activities. He spent his youth listening to old records. Mac acquired a $3.98 mail-order guitar and began entertaining at local events. In 1944, Mac began his professional career playing the upright bass for the Cumberland Mountain Folks. Mac became a vocalist and guitar player for Lester Flatt and Earl Scruggs's Foggy Mountain Boys and later joined Bill Monroe's Blue Grass Boys. In 1951, he released his first hit, "'Tis Sweet to Be Remembered." During the 1950s, Wiseman worked as the A&R executive and director for the country division of Dot Records. In 1958, he became a founder and board member for the Country Music Association. From 1966 to 1970, Mac helped to revitalize the *Wheeling Jamboree.* Mac Wiseman was known as the "Voice with a Heart." He was elected to the Bluegrass Hall of Honor (1993), Atlanta Country Music Hall of Fame (1994), and Country Music Hall of Fame (2014).

JODY REYNOLDS. Rockabilly songwriter and performer Jody Reynolds (1932–2008) was born in Denver, Colorado. Jody's most famous composition was "Endless Sleep" (1956). The song was rejected by several record companies because the lyrics were too depressing. Eventually, Demon Records accepted a demo of the song after Jody agreed to change the ending so that the girl was saved from drowning. In 1958, "Endless Sleep" was number five on the Billboard Hot 100. The record sold more than a million copies. Jody was elected to the Rockabilly Hall of Fame (1999). He loved writing songs and smoking cigars. We lived in nearby communities and became fast friends when he received my gift of Cuban cigars for his 75th birthday.

JODY REYNOLDS

Two

BARN DANCE PROGRAMS

**WLS NATIONAL BARN DANCE
SOUVENIR PROGRAM.** WLS
was originally owned by Sears,
Roebuck in Chicago, Illinois,
and was an acronym for the
World's Largest Store. The
National Barn Dance became
one of the first country music
radio programs in America. The
show was originally broadcast on
April 19, 1924, the first Saturday
that WLS went on the air. In
1925, WLS claimed to have
the first live studio audience.
In 1928, the station was sold to
The Prairie Farmer magazine.
In 1931, the show moved to
a 1,200-seat theater for two
Saturday evening programs. In
1932, the *National Barn Dance*
was broadcast on NBC on more
than 30 stations from coast to
coast. Beginning in 1949, the
show was televised on ABC-TV.

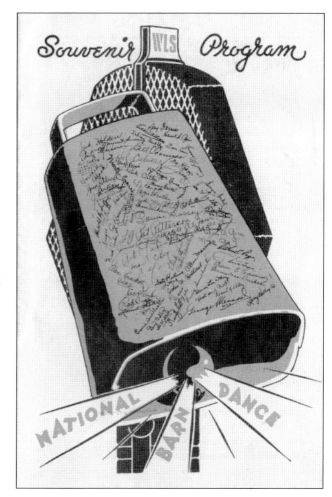

WLS National Barn Dance Cast, October, I

WLS National Barn Dance Cast, October 1944. ABC purchased WLS and canceled the *National Barn Dance* in 1959. The station's country music format was replaced by a new genre of music called rock and roll. The *National Barn Dance* then moved to WGN but went off the air in 1968.

BRADLEY KINCAID, "THE KENTUCKY MOUNTAIN BOY." William Bradley Kincaid (1895–1989), known as "the Kentucky Mountain Boy," was born in Port Leavall, Garrand County, Kentucky. From 1926 to 1931, he was a regular performer on the *National Barn Dance.* During that period, Bradley received more than 100,000 fan letters each year. He was a prolific songwriter who also collected mountain and folk songs. Kincaid published 13 songbooks that sold nearly half a million copies. He was famous for his "Houn' Dog Guitar," which was sold by Sears, Roebuck and is prized by collectors today. Kincaid later moved to the WLW *Midwest Hayride,* where he received 40,000 fan letters during his first month on the program. He became a member of the *Grand Ole Opry* around 1946 and retired in 1950. Bradley was elected to the Nashville Songwriters Hall of Fame (1971) and the Kentucky Music Hall of Fame (2002).

BRADLEY KINCAID
"The Kentucky Mountain Boy"

BRADLEY KINCAID POSTER. Bradley Kincaid played in concert at the Grand Theater in Union City, Indiana, on Wednesday and Thursday, October 26 and 27, 1938.

KARL AND HARTY. Karl Davis and Hartford Connecticut "Harty" Taylor were known as the Renfro Boys. They appeared on the *National Barn Dance* during the 1930s and 1940s. Karl wrote "Kentucky" and "I'm Just Here to Get My Baby Out of Jail," both of which were hit records for the Blue Sky Boys and the Everly Brothers.

SLIM MILLER. This photograph of Homer E. "Slim" Miller (1895–1962) was taken when he appeared on the *National Barn Dance*. When the Renfro Valley Project was first announced, many people thought it would take place. John Lair's vision was to create a barn dance venue in rural Renfro Valley, Kentucky. He promised that when the "big barn" was built, Slim would fiddle the opening tune on the first broadcast. Slim waited for 10 years until Lair's promise finally came true. He became "Dance Fiddler Number One" on the program. Slim was an everyday person who said he wouldn't get "too big fer his britches."

ARKIE WOODCHOPPER. Luther Ossenbrink (1906–1981), later known as Arkansas "Arkie" Woodchopper, was born in the Ozarks near Knob Noster, Missouri. There he chopped wood and "rode leather all day long." Arkie performed on the *National Barn Dance* from about 1930 to 1959. He was one of the three most popular acts on the program. The *WLS Family Album* of 1938 reported that Arkie loved to laugh and that "some of the boys found it was fun to make him laugh in the middle of a song, inventing some of the most outlandish stunts to accomplish this. Since then, Arkie's laugh has been heard coast to coast." He was "Manhandled. Wrapped in bandages. Sheet music set afire. Guitar pulled out of tune. Shoes unlaced. And he laughed and sang right through it all."

CUMBERLAND RIDGE RUNNERS. This photograph of the Cumberland Ridge Runners includes, from left to right, (first row) John Lair (harmonica) and Linda Parker (banjo), who was known as the "Sunbonnet Girl"; (second row) Slim Miller (fiddle), Karl Davis (mandolin), Red Foley (bass), and Hank Taylor (guitar).

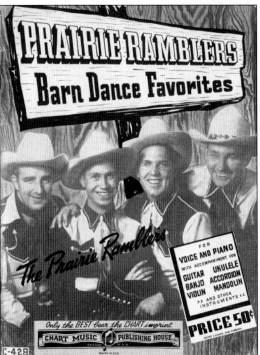

PRAIRIE RAMBLERS. This photograph of the Prairie Ramblers includes, from left to right, Jack Taylor, Chick Hurt, Salty Holmes, and Alan Crockett. The group was originally formed during the early 1930s as the Kentucky Ramblers. In 1932, the group joined the *National Barn Dance.*

PRAIRIE RAMBLERS, BARN DANCE FAVORITES. "Happy" Jack Taylor was born in Summer Shade, Kentucky, and was an original member of the group. He played bass and tenor banjo. Charles "Chick" Hurt (1905–1967) was born in Willow Shade, Kentucky, and was also an original group member. He played tenor banjo and mandolin. Salty Holmes (1910–1970) was born in Glasgow, Kentucky. He was a multi-instrumentalist and was known as the "maestro of the harmonica." In 1938, Alan Crockett joined the group to replace Tex Atchison on fiddle. Pictured from left to right are Jack Taylor, Alan Crockett, Chick Hurt, and Salty Holmes.

JENNY LOU CARSON. Virginia Lucille Overstake, later known as Jenny Lou Carson (1915–1978), was born in Decatur, Illinois. In 1932, she began performing on the *National Barn Dance* with her two sisters, Evelyn, also known as Judy Martin (1917–1951), and Eva Aliane (1918–1951). They were known as the "Three Little Maids." Carson was a prolific songwriter. Her catalog of 170 songs included "Jealous Heart," "Don't Rob Another Man's Castle," and "Let Me Go Lover." She was inducted as a member of the Nashville Songwriters Hall of Fame (1971).

SCOTTY AND LULU BELLE, VOGUE RECORD OF "IN THE DOG HOUSE NOW," 1947. Scott Greene "Scotty" Wiseman (1909–1981) and Myrtle Eleanor "Lulu Belle" Cooper (1913–1999) were the most popular act of the *National Barn Dance* during the 1930s. They married in 1934 and became known by fans as the "Hayloft Sweethearts." Scotty and Lulu Belle became regulars on the WLW *Midwest Hayride* in 1940. They appeared in several movies, including *Shine on Harvest Moon* (1938), *Village Barn Dance* (1940), and *National Barn Dance* (1944). The couple retired from showbusiness in 1958 and went on to new careers. Scotty began teaching, and Lulu Belle served in the North Carolina House of Representatives (1975–1978). Scotty was elected to the Nashville Songwriters Hall of Fame (1971). His compositions included "Have I Told You Lately that I Love You," "Mountain Dew," and "Remember Me (When the Candle Lights Are Gleaming)."

GEORGIE GOEBEL. George Goebel (later Gobel), the "Little Cowboy" (1919–1991), was born in Chicago, Illinois. He auditioned and appeared on the *National Barn Dance* in 1932. Georgie was the youngest and one of the most beloved members of the cast. After World War II, George began appearing in movies and an award-winning TV variety show.

THE ALKA-SELTZER NATIONAL BARN DANCE

Meet the radio artists who entertain you every Saturday night, bringing you a full hour of favorite music, singing and good wholesome fun.

Front row: Seated, Pat Buttram, Eddie Peabody, and Arkie; standing, Henry Burr and Joe Kelly. Second row: Hoosier Hot Shots, Ann, Pat and Judy, Bob Ballantine, Dinning Sisters, Prairie Ramblers. Third row: Hayloft Octette. Fourth, fifth and sixth rows: Jack Holden, the Hayloft Orchestra, and the Alka-Seltzer Barn Dance Directors.

Every Saturday Night—Coast-to-Coast—79 NBC Red Network Stations

THE *ALKA SELTZER NATIONAL BARN DANCE.* In 1933, Alka Seltzer printed sponsorships and endorsements for the *National Barn Dance.*

35

"Tune In Warp's." Pictured is a postcard advertisement from Warp's invites listeners to tune in to the WLS *National Barn Dance* every Saturday night at 7:30 Central Standard Time at 890 on the radio dial. In 1924, Harold Warp drove his Model T from Nebraska to Chicago with a patent for Flex-O-Glass. He had developed a special window material for his family chicken coops. Today, the company has three large plants and is a leader in the plastics industry.

Spring Hill Nurseries. Shown at left is a photograph of Red Foley and His Saddle Pals, appearing on WLS, sent with best wishes from Spring Hill Nurseries. Red Foley and His Saddle Pals also appeared in *The Pioneers*, a 1941 Western film featuring Tex Ritter.

PURINA'S GRAND OLE OPRY. The *Grand Ole Opry*, in Nashville, Tennessee, was first broadcast on WSM-AM 650 on November 28, 1925. Jesse Donald "Uncle Jimmy" Thompson was a 77-year-old fiddler who played the first tune on the WSM *Barn Dance*. George D. Hay (the "Solemn Old Judge") also appeared on the program.

UNCLE DAVE MACON. David Harrison "Uncle Dave" Macon (1870–1952) was born in Smart Station, Tennessee. He was the son of Confederate captain John Macon. In 1884, the family moved to Nashville. A year later, he learned to play banjo. In 1921, Uncle Dave began his professional music career. On July 8, 1924, fiddler Sid Harkreader and he made their first recordings for Vocalion in New York City. He later recorded for Bluebird, Brunswick, Decca, and Montgomery Ward.

SONGS AND STORIES

of

At Age of Sweet Sixteen

Uncle Dave Macon

SONGS AND STORIES OF UNCLE DAVE MACON. Macon performed on the first WSM *Barn Dance* show and became the program's first major star. He remained on the *Opry* until his death. Uncle Dave was elected to the Country Music Hall of Fame (1966) and was known as the "Grandfather of Country Music."

SEASON'S GREETINGS from THE PICKARD?
Dad, Ruth, Ma, Bubb, Charley
Little Letsey (On the Piano)
Ann (On the Floor)

THE PICKARD FAMILY. Research reveals a fascinating history of these early country music performers. There are two accounts regarding how Obediah "Obed" Pickard met George Hay, who was "inventor" of the *Grand Ole Opry*. The traditional story was published by the *Tennessean* on October 28, 1927. The article reported that "the accidental death of one of his daughters . . . brought Mr. Pickard to the studios of WSM. He came first to express his appreciation of a message which reached him while he was traveling in Virginia notifying him of the terrible accident." Obed's visit to WSM was the catalyst that resulted in his friendship with George Hay. Charlie Pickard (one of Obed's sons) told a different story. Charlie said that his father met George Hay at his uncle's bank in Nashville. Hay was talking to the uncle about starting a program like the *National Barn Dance* when Obed walked into the bank. The banker recommended that Hay audition his brother. Obed told Hay that he had once performed for Admiral Dewey in Manila. Hay was sufficiently impressed that he asked Obed to perform on the *Opry*. The Pickard Family first appeared on the *Opry* in May 1927. They were a popular singing group. They later moved to the WLS *National Barn Dance* and other cities around the country. The family finally moved to Hollywood, where they appeared in several low-budget Western movies and hosted a television program during the early 1950s.

THE WILBURN CHILDREN. This is a beautiful portrait of a legendary country music family. Benjamin "Pop" Wilburn was a disabled World War I veteran from Hardy, Arkansas. Like many rural Americans, during the Great Depression, he worked odd jobs to feed his family. One day, he saw a family whose car had broken down and who paid for repairs by singing and playing music for tips. Shortly thereafter, Pop ordered instruments from a Sears catalog and taught his children to play. On December 24, 1937, the Wilburn children (Lester, Leslie, and Geraldine) made their first performance on a street corner in Thayer, Missouri, playing guitar, fiddle, mandolin, and ukulele. A couple of years later, Pop and his children traveled to Birmingham, Alabama, for a talent contest hosted by Roy Acuff, the "King of Country Music," but arrived too late to enter the event. Pop and his children waited at the stage door for Acuff to exit. When he appeared, the children sang one of Acuff's favorite hymns. He was so impressed that he arranged for the children to appear on the *Opry*. In 1940, the Wilburn children became members of the *Opry* for six months but were forced to leave the program because of child labor laws. Geraldine married and left the group. Her younger brothers Teddy and Doyle joined Lester and Leslie. They regularly appeared on KWKH's *Louisiana Hayride*. After the group disbanded, Teddy and Doyle entered military service during Korea. After their discharge, Webb Pierce (whom they had met at the *Louisiana Hayride*) asked Teddy and Doyle to join him in Nashville, where they were a popular duo from the 1950s through the 1970s. Their syndicated television show from 1963 to 1974, the *Wilburn Brothers Show*, helped launch Loretta Lynn and the Osborne Brothers. They were inducted into the Arkansas Entertainers Hall of Fame (2008). (Courtesy of Jason Wilburn.)

ASHER SIZEMORE AND LITTLE JIMMIE. Asher Sizemore (1906–1975) and his son, Little Jimmie (1927–2014), appeared on the *Grand Old Opry* from 1933 through the mid-1940s. They started singing together when Little Jimmie was about five years old. Asher and Jimmie published and marketed a series of mail-order Health and Home Songs. They also made transcription recordings that were syndicated to radio stations in the Midwest and South.

PEE WEE KING AND HIS R.C.A.-VICTOR GOLDEN WEST COWBOYS. Julius Frank Anthony Kuczynski (1914–2000), whose stage name was "Pee Wee King," was born in Abrams, Wisconsin. During his youth, he learned to play accordion and became a professional polka musician. During the 1930s, he toured and appeared with Gene Autry in movies that included *Gold Mine in the Sky* (1938). He joined the *Grand Ole Opry* in 1937. Pee Wee formed the Golden West Cowboys. At various times, the band included Eddy Arnold, Cowboy Copas, Minnie Pearl, Ernest Tubb, and Redd Steward. In 1948, Pee Wee and Redd composed and recorded "The Tennessee Waltz." Their other hit records included "Bonaparte's Retreat" and "Slow Poke." He was inducted into the Nashville Songwriters Hall of Fame (1970) and Country Music Hall of Fame (1974).

BILL CARLISLE. William Tolliver "Bill" Carlisle (1908–2003) was born in Wakefield, Kentucky. He began performing with his older brother Cliff Carlisle during the 1920s. Carlisle earned the nickname "Jumpin' Bill" from his leaps on stage. When Cliff retired about 1950, Bill formed the Carlisles and was a member of the *Grand Ole Opry* from about 1953 until his death. He was elected to the Country Music Hall of Fame (2002).

COWBOY COPAS. Pictured standing in the back, second from left, Lloyd Estel "Cowboy" Copas (1913–1963) was born in Blue Creek, Ohio. He began performing at 14 on WLW and WKRC in Cincinnati. In 1940, Cowboy moved to Knoxville, Tennessee, and appeared with the Gold Star Rangers on WNOX. In 1943, he replaced Eddy Arnold as the vocalist with Pee Wee King's Golden West Cowboys and began performing on the *Grand Ole Opry*. His first hit record was "Filipino Baby" in 1946. In 1960, "Alabam" was released on Starday Records and became his biggest hit. On March 5, 1963, Copas died in a plane crash with Patsy Cline, Hawkshaw Hawkins, and pilot Randy Hughes, who was his son-in-law and Patsy's manager. The Piper Comanche encountered severe weather and crashed near Camden, Tennessee, en route from a benefit for disc jockey "Cactus Jack" Call, who had recently died in an automobile accident. He was inducted into America's Old Time Country Music Hall of Fame (2004).

GORDON TERRY. Gordon Terry (1931–2006) was born in Decatur, Alabama. At age nine, he made two appearances on the *Grand Ole Opry* with his father, Floyd Terry and His Young 'Uns (1941). At age 14, Gordon won first place at the Alabama Fiddling Championship. In 1950, he became a member of the *Opry*. A year earlier, he was hired as the fiddler for Bill Monroe's Bluegrass Boys and recorded with the group until 1970. Terry moved to California and became a member of Town Hall Party in 1958. He appeared in several movies and television shows, including *Sky King*. Gordon later performed with Faron Young, on the *Johnny Cash Show*, and with Merle Haggard and Neil Young. Rhonda Thorson recalls that her father was extremely proud to have been the founder of ROPE (Reunion of Retired Entertainers) in 1983. Their goal was to develop a retirement home for the country music industry. Gordon was a charter member of the Fiddlers Hall of Fame (1981) and inducted into the Southern Legends Entertainment and Performing Arts Hall of Fame (2006). Be sure to drive safely along the Gordon Terry Parkway in Decatur, Alabama. Rhonda told me that her father was part of the *Johnny Cash Show* from 1958 to 1968. After he left the show, Gordon and Johnny "remained good friends, but June (Carter Cash) did not feel that Daddy was a good influence as you might imagine. When Daddy gave his life to Jesus in 1974, word got to Johnny through Mama Cash that Daddy had been 'saved.' Johnny called him the next evening and told him to grab his fiddle and get to Dallas! June had given permission for Daddy to join them again!" Out of curiosity, I called Larry Collins, wondering how Gordon Terry could have been such a bad influence on notorious bad boy Johnny Cash. Larry and his sister Lorrie (known as "The Collins Kids") were also members of the *Johnny Cash Show* during those years. He told me a story about touring Canada and performing in a large auditorium with a balcony. The Collins Kids opened the show and were followed by Gordon, who played fiddle tunes and sang his standard songs such as "Johnson's Old Grey Mule." During his set, a heckler in the balcony repeatedly yelled, "Get off the stage. You don't know what you're doing." (Gordon was tall, extremely athletic, and possessed the "Terry temper." His strength and swimming prowess resulted in an offer for him to play *Tarzan* in the movies.) After several rounds of heckling, Gordon put down his fiddle and bow, proceeded to the balcony, and pummeled the heckler. He then returned to the stage and was greeted by the audience with a standing ovation.

THE OAK RIDGE QUARTET. In 1943, Wally Fowler (1917–1994) formed a group called the Georgia Clodhoppers in Knoxville, Tennessee. The original members consisted of Wally Fowler, Curley Kinsey, Johnny New, and Lon "Deacon" Freeman. During World War II, the group was frequently asked to perform at the nuclear research facility in Oak Ridge, Tennessee. They played there so often that the group's name was changed to the Oak Ridge Quartet. They were members of the *Grand Ole Opry* and were known for their gospel songs. In 1957, Fowler sold the group's name to Smitty Gatlin in exchange for a gambling debt. Gatlin's record producer thought the name sounded too old fashioned, so the group became known as the Oak Ridge Boys.

WOC BARN DANCE FROLIC. The WOC *Barn Dance Frolic* originated in Davenport, Iowa, around 1931. A year later, the program moved to Des Moines, Iowa, where it broadcast over a sister station.

WLW Boone County Jamboree. The *Boone County Jamboree*, sometimes known as the *Midwest Hayride*, was broadcast on WLW-AM 700 every Saturday night from before 1937 through the early 1970s. The program became an NBC-TV summer replacement show from 1951 to 1956 and was on ABC-TV for the summers of 1957 to 1959. During the 1940s, the show's regular performers included the Delmore Brothers, Merle Travis, Red Foley, and Grandpa Jones, each of whom later became members of the Country Music Hall of Fame.

WLW Boone County Jamboree, Bigger and Better than Ever for 1940. "Every Saturday evening, this great company of top-notch entertainers packs them in at Cincinnati's Emery Auditorium for two and a half hours of fun and music. For millions of listeners, the two half-hour broadcasts each Saturday are the high spots of their radio week. Come and see the WLW *Boone County Jamboree* when you can; next summer, look for the WLW *Jamboree* at your State or County Fair." The *Boone County Jamboree* (later known as the *Midwestern Hayride*) was first broadcast live on radio each Saturday evening from about 1937 until the early 1970s.

DRIFTING PIONEERS' SONG FOLIO
No. 1, 1939. The Drifting Pioneers
appeared on the WLW *Boone
County Jamboree* from 1937 until the
beginning of World War II. The group
included Morris "Sleepy" Martin
(fiddle), Walter Brown (mandolin),
Bill Brown (bass), and Merle "Pappy"
Travis (guitar). The group made at
least one 78-rpm record on Gospel
Records of "Looking for a City"
and "Leave That Liar Alone."

WORLD'S ORIGINAL RADIO JAMBOREE. On
January 7, 1933, the *Wheeling Jamboree*
was first broadcast on WWVA-AM
1170 from Wheeling, West Virginia.
Three months later, there was a live-
audience premier of the world's original
WWVA *Wheeling Jamboree* at the
Capitol Theatre in Wheeling.

GRANDPA JONES. Louis Marshall "Grandpa" Jones (1913–1998) was born in Niagara, Kentucky. In 1936, he became a member of the *Wheeling Jamboree*. Grandpa was known for his claw hammer banjo playing and was famous for recordings such as "Old Rattler," "Mountain Dew," and his composition "Eight More Miles to Louisville." In 1969, he was an original cast member of *Hee Haw*. Grandpa was inducted into the Country Music Hall of Fame (1978) and the Kentucky Music Hall of Fame (2002).

DOC WILLIAMS AND THE BORDER RIDERS. From left to right are Milo Smik (1918–2006), Doc's fiddle playing brother, known as Cy Williams; Jessie Wanda Krupe, Doc's wife, known as Chickie Williams; blind accordionist Marion Martin; and Doc. Andrew John Smik Jr. (1914–2011), later known as Doc Williams, was born in Cleveland, Ohio, and raised in Kittanning, Pennsylvania. During the early 1930s, Doc made his professional debut with the Kansas Clodhoppers. In 1937, he formed Doc Williams and the Border Riders and began performing on WWVA. In 1939, he married Jessie Krupe (1919–2007). Doc Williams was inducted into the West Virginia Music Hall of Fame (2009).

WILMA LEE AND STONEY COOPER WITH THE CLINCH MOUNTAIN CLAN. Wilma Lee Leary (1923–2011) and Dale T. "Stoney" Cooper (1918–1977) were native to West Virginia. Stoney played fiddle and was a member of the Leary Family Singers, a gospel group that included Wilma Lee. The couple married in 1941. Wilma Lee and Stoney became members of the *Wheeling Jamboree* in 1947. They moved to the *Grand Ole Opry* in 1957. Along with the Clinch Mountain Clan, Wilma Lee and Stoney were a popular act from the 1940s through the 1960s. They performed traditional gospel and mountain songs. In 1965, they were a featured act in the movie *Country Music on Broadway*.

TOBY STROUD'S WYOMING RANCH GANG. This picture of Toby Stroud and his Wyoming Ranch Gang on WWVA includes Toby Stroud (guitar), Buck Ryan (fiddle), and Bill Bailey (mandolin).

WWVA Smile Sisters. April and Patricia Obrenovich were known as the Smile Sisters. The girls performed on the *Wheeling Jamboree* from 1941 to 1944. The sisters then moved to Phoenix, Arizona, where they continued their radio and personal appearance career.

Renfro Valley Barn Dance in Mount Vernon, Kentucky. The *Renfro Valley Barn Dance* is a country music stage and radio program that debuted on WLW in Cincinnati, Ohio, in 1937. The show moved to Mount Vernon, Kentucky, in 1939. It continues to present live performances every Saturday evening.

THE OLD DOMINION BARN DANCE CAST. The *Old Dominion Barn Dance* was broadcast every Saturday night on WRVA in Richmond, Virginia, from November 1939 until 1964.

MARY WORKMAN. This is a photograph of Sunshine Sue and Her Rangers from an *Old Dominion Barn Dance* picture album. Mary Workman (1915–1979), whose stage name was "Sunshine Sue," began singing on the *Old Dominion Barn Dance* in December 1940. She was the "Femcee" or host of the program from 1946 to 1957.

SUNSHINE SUE *and her* RANGERS

Sam Workman, born in Mt. Zion, Iowa. Plays guitar and sings. First joined Rangers in 1935. Married, has beautiful wife, and three boys: Larry, age 5, Dick and Don (twins), age 2. — Irving Gurganus, born in Williamston, N. C. A fine fiddler and singer. Joined Rangers December 10, 1945. — Mary A. Workman, wife of John, known as "Sunshine Sue" in radio 13 years, plays accordion and sings, acts as Mistress of Ceremonies of Barn Dance. Her main interest is "Billie Boy." — John Workman, "Big Sugarfoot," married Sue right after they finished high school. Plays bass and sings. Business manager of the act. — Irvin L. Kersey, "Pokey." Born in Richmond, Va. First played music at the age of 9. Plays "store-bought" guitar and sings. Joined Rangers September, 1944.

CRAZY JOE

Cousin Crazy Joe Maphis has been a radio entertainer since the age of 12. A native of Suffolk, Va., later moving to West Virginia. Has picked and sung with Sue, John and Sam Workman since 1940. Took time out for 3 years overseas duty for Uncle Sam. One of the original members of the Old Dominion Barn Dance cast. Has been featured on most of the larger Barn Dance shows in the country. He is pictured here with his latest—Cindy the 1923 Ford, which he brings right out on the stage on Saturday nights.

JOE MAPHIS. Otis Wilson "Joe" Maphis (1921–1986) was born in Suffolk, Virginia. Joe was known as the "King of the Strings"—in addition to his double-neck Mosrite guitar, he mastered the fiddle, banjo, and other stringed instruments. This *Old Dominion Barn Dance* photograph was taken around 1946.

THE SADDLE SWEETHEARTS. Rose Schetrompf (later Rose Lee Maphis) and Mary Klick performed as the Saddle Sweethearts. Rose was born in 1922 on a farm near Baltimore. Mary was from Hagerstown, Maryland. They began their radio career during the late 1930s. The Saddle Sweethearts appeared on the *Old Fashioned Barn Dance* in on KMOX in St. Louis, Missouri. They moved to Richmond to join the *Old Dominion Barn Dance* in 1945. Rose left the Saddle Sweethearts during the late 1940s.

THE SADDLE SWEETHEARTS

The Saddle Sweethearts, Rose and Mary, two lovely young ladies, who pick and sing just as pretty as they look. On the left is Rose Schetrompf, who was born in Baltimore, Md. Started in radio at the age of 15. Plays guitar and does very nice solo work as well as harmony. On the right is Mary Klick, born in Hagerstown, Md. Started in radio in 1939, plays guitar and bass fiddle. The girls are nationally famous in radio, and joined the Old Dominion Barn Dance family in July, 1948.

CHESTER ATKIN. Chester Burton "Chet" Atkins (1924–2001) was born in Luttrell, Tennessee. This photograph was included in an *Old Dominion Barn Dance* picture album from the late 1940s. Chet was known as "Mr. Guitar." He was also famous as a record producer and inventor of the "Nashville Sound." Chet was elected to the Country Music Hall of Fame (1973), Academy of Country Music Pioneers (1982), Georgia Music Hall of Fame (1995), Atlanta Country Music Hall of Fame (1999), Rock and Roll Hall of Fame (2002), and Musicians Hall of Fame (2009). He received 14 Grammy awards, including the Lifetime Achievement Award.

FOREMAN PHILLIPS COUNTY BARN DANCE PHOTOGRAPH. Bert A. "Foreman" Phillips (1897–1968) started the *Los Angeles County Barn Dance* in 1941. His first venue was the Venice Pier in Santa Monica, California. He also organized barn dance programs in Compton, Culver City, the Riverside Rancho in Griffith Park, and Baldwin Park, California. Foreman was a disc jockey who is often credited with inventing the term "Western swing." From left to right, this photograph includes Red Murrell (1921–2001), unidentified, Tex Atchison (1912–1982), Les "Carrot Top" Anderson (1921–2001), unidentified, Glen Troutman (later known as Glen Glenn, born in 1934), Gary Lambert (1936–1982), Clarence White (1944–1973), and Roland White (born 1938).

SPADE COOLEY, TEX WILLIAMS, AND SMOKEY ROGERS. From left to right are Spade Cooley (1910–1969), Tex Williams (1917–1985), and Smokey Rogers (1917–1983). Donnell Clyde "Spade" Cooley was born in Grand, Oklahoma. He was known as the "King of Western Swing." In 1944, *Billboard* magazine reported that Spade Cooley performed at the Venice Pier Ballroom for 74 consecutive weeks. His dances drew an average attendance of 5,000–7,000. Cooley appeared in 38 Western films and was a stand-in for cowboy actor Roy Rogers. An estimated 75 percent of all televisions in the Los Angeles area were tuned into *The Hoffman Hayride* every Saturday night on KTLA-TV. In 1960, Spade was honored with a star on the Hollywood Walk of Fame.

SPADE COOLEY CONCERT, EUGENE ARMORY, 1948. The boxing-style poster promotes a March 10, 1948, concert in Eugene, Oregon. In March 1961, Spade's wife of 15 years, Ella Mae Evans, filed for divorce. The reasons included Ella's admission of an affair with Roy Rogers during the early 1950s as well as Spade's numerous infidelities, heavy drinking, and abusive behavior. A month later, Spade attacked and murdered his wife. He was convicted of first-degree murder and sentenced to life in prison. In 1969, Spade was scheduled for release from prison. He had been a model prisoner and was suffering from a severe heart condition. A few months prior to his scheduled release, Spade was asked to perform a benefit concert for deputy police officers in Oakland, California. After receiving a standing ovation for his performance, Spade went backstage for an intermission and suffered a fatal heart attack.

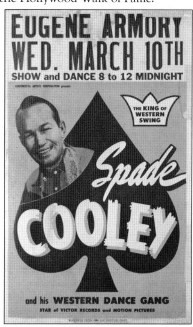

GLENN TROUTMAN and GARY LAMBERT

GLEN TROUTMAN AND GARY LAMBERT. Glen Troutman, who later changed his name to Glen Glenn, was born in Joplin, Missouri, in 1934. Gary Lambert (1936–2018) was born in Southern California. They formed a country duo called the Missouri Mountain Boys. Glen sang and Gary was a gifted guitar player. After attending an Elvis Presley concert in 1956, Glen decided to pursue a rockabilly career. He received a Rockabilly Hall of Fame Lifetime Achievement Award (2005). Gary and Eddie Cochran recorded *Guitar Pickin' Rarities*, released by Sun Jay Records in 1992. Gary proudly remembered touring with the Everly Brothers. He was asked to join Phil and Don because his finger-style guitar was reminiscent of their father, Ike Everly.

GARY LAMBERT AND GUITAR GREATS. This photograph was taken by Jeanne Lambert, Gary's wife, at Studio A in Nashville, Tennessee, around 1968. From left to right are Joe Maphis, Jody Maphis, Gary Lambert, Chet Atkins, and Jerry Reed. Gary also played guitar in Wynn Stewart's house band for appearances in Southern California.

54

CHIPPEWA

VALLEY

JAMBOREE

WEAU

WEAU CHIPPEWA VALLEY JAMBOREE.
According to an article in the July
4, 1976, *Eau Claire Leader-Telegram*,
Scotty and Maggie Swan originated
the WEAU *Chippewa Valley Barn
Dance* in Eau Claire, Wisconsin,
in 1948. The program continued
through the early 1950s.

MAGGIE AND SCOTTIE SWAN. Magdalen
"Maggie" Culbert (1921–1995) and
Jules "Scottie" Swan (1918–1989)
stated that Maggie sang cover songs
of Kitty Wells, Patsy Cline, and other
female singers of the day. Scottie Swan
often played a black Gibson double-
neck guitar. The couple performed
from the late 1940s until about 1981.

CBS RADIO NETWORK		
RADIO STUDIO B	SUNDAY	
6121 SUNSET BLVD., HOLLYWOOD, CALIF.	DECEMBER	

CBS RADIO NETWORK
RADIO STUDIO B
6121 SUNSET BLVD., HOLLYWOOD, CALIF.

SAL HEPATICA presents
"HOLLYWOOD BARN DANCE"
Starring
JIMMY WAKELY
Featuring
ROBERTA LINN

SUNDAY
DECEMBER
14
1952
3:30-4 p.m.
Doors Close
at 3:20 p.m.

№ 1410

HOLLYWOOD BARN DANCE TICKET. The *Hollywood Barn Dance* was hosted by Cottonseed Clark. The show aired from 1943 to 1952 and was broadcast from CBS Studios in Hollywood, California. It replaced *Melody Ranch* while Gene Autry was serving in the Army Air Force during World War II.

HOLLYWOOD BARN DANCE   RADIO STATION KNX, LOS ANGELES

HOLLYWOOD BARN DANCE PHOTOGRAPH. The *Hollywood Barn Dance*, broadcast by KNX in Los Angeles, California, is pictured around 1948 with, from left to right, Foy Willing, Jimmie Dean, Al Sloey, Bart Roth, Cliffie Stonehead, Maury Styne, Cottonseed Clark, Johnny Bond, Tex Lighter, Art Denzel, June "Sunshine Girl" Widener, Colleen Summers (later Mary Ford), Virginia Barles, and Ozie Water.

Where Can You Find...

A Writer—
ANDREWS SISTERS "EIGHT TO THE BAR RANCH"; CBS HOLLYWOOD BARN DANCE; THE LAW WEST OF THE PECOS, with WALTER BRENNAN

Poet—
BRUSHWOOD POETRY—Leeds Publishers

Radio Producer—
LAW WEST OF THE PECOS; CBS HOLLYWOOD BARN DANCE; PRODUCED ANDREWS SISTERS ORIGINAL "EIGHT TO THE BAR RANCH."

Creator—
CREATED HOLLYWOOD BARN DANCE, ANDREWS SISTERS "EIGHT TO THE BAR RANCH" and THE LAW WEST OF THE PECOS.

Actor—
MASTE OF CEREMONIES HOLLYWOOD BARN DANCE AND TWO OTHER SHOWS ON KNX CBS WEST COAST.

Song Writer—
TEXAS BLUES; LOVE THAT WE ONCE KNEW; I LEARNED TO LOVE YOU TOO LATE; and numerous other Western and folk songs.

An Outstanding Authority on Western, Hillbilly and American Folklore
Writer, Producer and MC of "Rhythm Range" for World Transcription

NOW RECORDING ALBUM OF BRUSHWOOD POETRY FOR DECCA RECORDS

Combined in One Personality

COTTONSEED CLARK
Is Your Man!

Management
MAURICE DUKE

COTTONSEED CLARK. Slim Clark Fulks (1909–1992), known as "Cottonseed Clark," was born in Paris, Texas. Clark began his radio career hosting a weekly hometown program featuring local talent. The program took place on WRR in Dallas, Texas, in 1929. He continued as a radio broadcaster in Texas through the 1930s. During the early 1940s, Cottonseed moved to Los Angeles, where CBS Radio asked him to create a replacement show for Gene Autry's *Melody Ranch*. After less than two weeks of planning, Clark debuted as host and producer for *Hollywood Barn Dance* on December 4, 1943. Cottonseed remained as the program's host until 1950 before moving to radio station KVSM in San Mateo, California. He wrote *Cottonseed Clark's Brushwood Poetry* and appeared as an actor in *Smoky River Serenade* (1947) and *Arkansas Swing* (1948). Cottonseed Clark recorded his poetry on RCA and Decca Records. As a songwriter, his composition "Texarkana Baby" became one of Eddy Arnold's early hits, reaching number one on Billboard's Best-Selling Folk Records in August 1948.

FOY WILLING AND THE RIDERS OF THE PURPLE SAGE. This photograph includes, from left to right, Al Sloey, Foy Willing, and Scotty Herrell. Foy Lopez Willingham (1914–1978) was born in Bosque County, Texas. He received his first guitar while in junior high school. At the age of 15, Foy performed three times a week on WACO-AM in Waco, Texas. In the early 1940s, Foy moved to California to work with Jimmy Wakely and the Saddle Pals. In 1942, Al Sloey and Foy formed the Riders of the Purple Sage. In 1943, his group became the stage band for *Hollywood Barn Dance*. In 1944, "Texas Blues" became their first hit recording. Foy appeared in 32 Western movies with stars that included Monty Hale, Roy Rogers, Charles Starrett, and Jimmy Wakely. The group disbanded in 1952.

JIMMY WAKELY AND *HOLLYWOOD BARN DANCE* CAST. From left to right are (first row) Jimmy Wakely and Colleen Summers (later known as Mary Ford); (second row) Johnny Bond, Cotton Thompson, Tex Atchison, and Dick Reinhart.

LOUISIANA HAYRIDE WITH ELVIS PRESLEY. This *Louisiana Hayride* photograph shows Elvis Presley singing "That's All Right Mama" along with the Blue Moon Boys and announcer Frank Page on October 16, 1954. The group members included Elvis Presley (1935–1977), Scotty Moore (1931–2016) on guitar, and Bill Black (1926–1955) on bass.

HOMETOWN JAMBOREE. The *Hometown Jamboree* was hosted by Cliffie Stone (also known as "Stonehead") and broadcast from 1949 to 1959 on KXLA in Pasadena, California. The photograph includes, standing from left to right, Harold Hensley (fiddle), Speedy West (steel guitar), Eddie Kirk, Tennessee Ernie Ford, Bucky Tibbs, Billy Liebert (accordion), and Herman the Hermit (banjo).

DINNER BELL GANG. This photograph of the Dinner Bell Gang "On the Air KXLA" includes, from left to right, (seated) the Armstrong twins; (standing) Harold Hensley, Billy Liebert, Eddie Kirk, Judy Hayden, Cliffie Stone, Herman the Hermit, Merle Travis with his Bigsby solid-body guitar, and Tennessee Ernie Ford. The photograph erroneously places Tennessee Ernie's name below Merle Travis and Merle Travis's name under Tennessee Ernie.

Merle Travis and Hometown Jamboree Cast Members. This photograph includes, from left to right, Tex Atchison (fiddle), Merle Travis (1917–1983), Tex Ann (1922–1998), "Red" Murrell (1921–2001), and Clifford Stone (1917–1998).

Herman the Hermit. Clifford Herman "Herman the Hermit" Snyder (1884–1964) received his big break when he was hired as an extra for the 1930 filming of *The Big Trail*. The movie featured John Wayne in his first leading role. After playing "Oh Suzanna" on his banjo for the film crew during evening campfires, he was asked to play the tune on the film score. Stuart Hamblen, a popular radio host, went to the movie and heard Snyder's banjo on the soundtrack. He tracked down Snyder and asked him to join his radio show band. Snyder showed up with the long hair and full beard that he had grown for the film, and Hamblen christened him "Herman the Hermit." When Snyder later got his son Clifford a job playing bass in the band, Hamblen nicknamed the boy "Cliffie Stonehead." The boy eventually shortened his stage name to Cliffie Stone.

TOWN HALL PARTY TICKET AND PENNANT. *Town Hall Party* was produced by William B. Wagnon Jr. and originated from the old town hall building at 400 South Long Beach Boulevard in Compton, California. Wagnon acquired a lease on the building from Burt "Foreman" Phillips, who had been promoting one of his barn dance programs from the same location. The ballroom accommodated an estimated 3,000. *Town Hall Party* began broadcasting in 1951. The show became a regional television program in 1953 over KTTV Channel 11 in Los Angeles, airing on Saturdays from 10:00 p.m. to 1:00 a.m. In 1958, the newly opened Showboat Hotel in Las Vegas, Nevada, produced *Town Hall Party* stage shows. The final show at the Compton Town Hall aired on January 14, 1961.

TEX RITTER

TEX RITTER. Woodward Maurice "Tex" Ritter (1905–1974) was born in Murvaul, Texas. In 1928, he began singing cowboy songs on KPRC in Houston, Texas. In 1931, Tex traveled to New York City, where he performed as cowboy Cord Elam in *Green Grow the Lilacs* (which later served as the basis for *Oklahoma*) and several other Broadway productions. In 1933, he began a recording career that spanned four decades. In 1936, Tex moved to Los Angeles, and he appeared in more than 70 Western movies. Tex Ritter became a featured performer on *Town Hall Party*. From 1958 to 1961, he was host of *Ranch Party*, a syndicated television version of *Town Hall Party*. During this time, young Larry Collins often rode in the back seat of Tex Ritter's Cadillac to performances. Tex enjoyed telling stories about aborigine headhunters and a variety of other tall tales. Larry recalls that Tex loved Jim Beam whiskey and smoking Camels with ashes that reached the end of his cigarette. Tex was also the father of John Ritter, who played Jack Tripper on the ABC sitcom *Three's Company*. Tex moved to Nashville in 1965. He became the Republican candidate for the US Senate in 1970. His lifetime achievements include induction into the Country Music Hall of Fame (1964), Nashville Songwriters Hall of Fame (1971), Academy of Country Music Pioneers (1974), Western Music Association Hall of Fame (1989), and Texas Country Music Hall of Fame (1998).

MERLE TRAVIS. This photograph, from Gary Lambert's estate, was probably taken during the early 1950s in a Southern California bar. Merle is playing his Gibson Super 400 guitar. A sign on the wall reads, "Plase [sic] keep your 'buts' off floor orders from fire chief." Merle Robert Travis (1917–1983) was born in Rosewood, Kentucky. His father was a coal miner. Merle composed "Sixteen Tons," "Dark as a Dungeon," and other coal mine songs. He was a legendary Kentucky thumb picker whose style became known as "Travis picking." Merle's guitar playing was an inspiration to Chet Atkins, Doc Watson, and legions who followed him. In the late 1940s, Merle moved from Cincinnati to Los Angeles, where he became a regular performer on the *Hollywood Barn Dance*, *Town Hall Party*, and other local television programs. He was also a studio musician who played on nearly all of Hank Thompson's recording sessions. Travis appeared in several films but is best remembered for singing "Re-Enlistment Blues" in *From Here to Eternity* (1953), a Frank Sinatra movie that won eight Academy Awards. He was elected to the Nashville Songwriters Hall of Fame (1970) and received the Academy of Country Music Pioneer Award (1974). He was inducted into the Country Music Hall of Fame (1977) and the Kentucky Music Hall of Fame (2002).

JOE AND ROSE LEE MAPHIS. Joe and Rose Lee Maphis met when both were regular performers on the *Old Dominion Barn Dance* in Richmond, Virginia. Joe moved to California in 1951. Rose Lee soon followed. They married in 1952. "Mr. and Mrs. Country Music" became regulars on *Town Hall Party*. During this period, Joe played guitar on the early recordings of Ricky Nelson, the Collins Kids, and Wanda Jackson. His movie contributions include *God's Little Acre*, *Thunder Road*, and *High Noon*, as well as the TV show *Bonanza*. Rose once stated that while Joe and she lived in Virginia, they usually performed in schools, churches, and public auditoriums. In California, they played in honky-tonk bars filled with cigarette smoke and loud music. After attending a Buck Owens performance at the Black Board in Bakersfield, Joe and Rose Lee were inspired to write "Dim Lights, Thick Smoke, and Loud Music." Joe and Rose Lee were inducted into the Mountain Maryland Music Hall of Fame (2017).

WESLEY AND MARILYN TUTTLE. Wesley Tuttle (1917–2003) was born in Lamar, Colorado. In 1947, he married Marilyn Myers (born 1925). Early in his career, Wesley joined Stuart Hamblen's band and sang on radio with the Sons of the Pioneers. He yodeled "The Silly Song" in Walt Disney's *Snow White and the Seven Dwarfs*. Wesley also appeared in several Western films, including *Song of the Sierras* with Jimmy Wakely (1946). In that movie, he sang "Detour," which became a million-selling record and his signature song. Wesley was the music director of *Town Hall Party*. Marilyn and Wes recorded many successful songs for Capitol Records. In 1954, their daughter Leslie died in a swimming pool accident. Later that year, Wesley was baptized in the same pool. The following year, he became a minister for the Church of Christ Ministries. During the next two decades, Wes and Marilyn participated in more than 175 revivals lasting from one to two weeks, performed more than 750 gospel concerts and recorded eight albums for Sacred and Christian Faith labels. Marilyn and Wes also operated a Christian book store for many years. In 1997, Wesley was inducted into the Western Music Association Hall of Fame. In 2002, Bear Family Records released a 5-CD, 1-DVD box set titled *Detour*, a tribute and compilation of Wes's recordings and transcriptions for Capitol Records. Wesley died the following year, but Marilyn (age 95) still enjoys singing her Western music!

THE COLLINS KIDS. The Collins Kids were original rockabilly superstars. Lawrencine May "Lorrie" Collins (1942–2018) and Larry Collins (born 1944) were born in Bad Water, Oklahoma. In 1954, they became regular performers on *Town Hall Party*. The Collins Kids were also featured on Tex Ritter's *Ranch Party*, a syndicated television version of *Town Hall Party* from 1957 to 1959, and *Star Route* (1964). Larry was a child prodigy and an incredible guitar player. His name is synonymous with the Mosrite double-neck guitar. Larry also cowrote "Delta Dawn" and "You're the Reason God Made Oklahoma." Lorrie was an extremely talented singer and rhythm guitar player. She was cast as Ricky Nelson's girlfriend and her identical twin in *The Adventures of Ozzie and Harriet* (1958). The Collins Kids performed at Madison Square Gardens and rockabilly festivals throughout the world. They are members of the Rockabilly Hall of Fame. Lorrie died in August 2018.

LARRY COLLINS AND RICO. Larry continues to perform at select rockabilly festivals and events in the United States and Spain. This photograph of Larry and his companion Rico was taken at Salvation Mountain near Niland, California (2017). Rico is a black-and-white Havanese that dines almost exclusively on chicken breast.

"JENKS" TEX CARMAN
Capital Recording Artist

TEX CARMAN. Jenks "Tex" Carman (1903–1968) was born in Hardinsburg, Kentucky. Tex claimed Cherokee ancestry and would sometimes wear an Indian headdress on stage. However, there is no evidence he possessed any Cherokee heritage. In 1929, Tex began recording and performing in Kentucky before moving to California, where he became a regular performer on Cliffie Stone's *Hometown Jamboree.* Tex later appeared on *Town Hall Party.* Apparently, Tex had no sense of rhythm and often played his Hawaiian laptop guitar out of tune. Wesley Tuttle was quoted as saying that Tex was the "worst musician in the world." Another story reported that Tex beat a son who untuned one of his guitar strings and refused to divulge which one. Tex was a notorious drinker and smoker and chewed tobacco. Johnny Western remarked that Tex would appear at a show half drunk, and there would be a bottle of liquor in his guitar case. Larry Collins recalls leaving on a tour with Joe Maphis and Tex Carman. Joe decided that Tex should ride with Larry and his father in their new Fleetwood Cadillac. As they were leaving the town hall parking lot in Compton, Tex spit "chew" between his legs on the back floor of the otherwise pristine car. Larry's father immediately removed Tex from the car and told Joe, "He's riding with you." Although he was neither a good singer nor an accomplished musician, Tex was a born entertainer. Larry said that Tex captivated the *Town Hall Party* audience, and women loved him.

THE CROSSROADS OF COUNTRY MUSIC. In 1955, Red Foley became host of *Ozark Jubilee*, a country music variety show. The program was broadcast every Saturday evening from the Jewell Theatre in Springfield, Missouri, on ABC-TV. The name of the show was later changed to *Country Music Jubilee* and finally *Jubilee USA*. The program aired 297 episodes over six years. Clyde Julian "Red" Foley (1910–1968) was born in Blue Lick, Kentucky. He was originally selected by a talent scout to become a member of the Cumberland Ridge Runners on the *National Barn Dance*. During the 1940s and 1950s, Red sold more than 25 million records. In 1951, Foley recorded "Peace in the Valley," a song that became one of the first gospel records to sell a million copies. As the host of *Ozark Jubilee*, he concluded each program with a song of faith and inspiration.

BRENDA LEE   ABC-TV OZARK JUBILEE   DECCA RECORDS

BRENDA LEE. Brenda Mae Tarpley, also known as "Brenda Lee," was born on December 11, 1944, in Atlanta, Georgia. In 1955, she made her first network appearance on *Ozark Jubilee*. At four feet, nine inches tall, she was nicknamed "Little Miss Dynamite" after she recorded the song "Dynamite" in 1957. During the 1960s, she recorded 47 charting songs. Only Elvis Presley, the Beatles, and Ray Charles surpassed this accomplishment. Her international record sales have exceeded 100 million. Brenda's biggest hits were "I'm Sorry" and "Rockin' 'Round the Christmas Tree." She was inducted into the Georgia Music Hall of Fame (1982), Atlanta Country Music Hall of Fame (1986), Country Music Hall of Fame (1997), and Rock and Roll Hall of Fame (2002).

Three

SILVER SCREEN
COUNTRY MUSIC STARS

TAKE ME BACK TO OKLAHOMA. From left to right, this lobby card features Tex Ritter, Bob Willis, and the Texas Playboys, including Leon McAuliffe (steel guitar), Johnny Lee Wills (banjo), Eldon Shamblin (guitar), Son Caz Lansford (bass), and Wayne Johnson (clarinet).

ARIZONA TRAIL. This *Arizona Trail* (1943) lobby card includes, from left to right, Jimmie Dean (guitar), Wesley Tuttle (left-handed guitar), Paul Sells (accordion), Fuzzy Knight, Johnny Bond, and Tex Ritter.

NIGHT TRAIN TO MEMPHIS. *Night Train to Memphis* (1946) starred Allan "Rocky" Lane and featured Roy Acuff (fiddle) and His Smokey Mountain Boys, including Sonny Day (accordion).

SONG OF THE SIERRAS. Jimmy Wakely starred in *Song of the Sierras* (1946) along with Wesley Tuttle and his Texas Stars, including Jack Rivers (guitar), Agapito Martinez (steel guitar), Stanley Ellison (accordion), and Jesse Ashlock (fiddle).

Smiley Burnette adds his barytone to the quartet's harmony!

GALLOPING THUNDER. Charles Starrett (1903–1986) appeared as the Durango Kid with Smiley Burnette in *Galloping Thunder* (1946). Other actors included Merle Travis (guitar) and the Broncho Busters.

HOLLYWOOD BARN DANCE. *Hollywood Barn Dance* (1947) included Ernest Tubb and his Texas Troubadours, including Jack Guthrie (1915–1948), Jack Drake (bass player and brother of Pete Drake, steel guitar legend), Jimmie Short (1916–1986), and Leon Short (1919–1988). Guthrie sang "Oakie Boogie," which became number three on the charts in 1947 and is considered by many to be on the list of the first rock and roll songs. None of the original *Hollywood Barn Dance* cast members appear in the movie.

BLAZING TRAIL. This is a lobby card for *Blazing Trail* (1949), featuring Charles Starrett (not pictured) as the Durango Kid. Pictured from left to right are Slim Duncan (fiddle), Smiley Burnette with one of his bizarre musical inventions, unidentified, Hank Penny (guitar), and unidentified. The unidentified musicians are not listed as movie cast members. (Courtesy of Shari Penny.)

Four

RADIO COWBOY AND HILLBILLY PERFORMERS

HAL LONE PINE. Harold John Breau (1916–1977), also known as "Hal Lone Pine," was born in Pea Cove, Maine. In 1938, he married Rita M. Cote (1921–2014), known as "Betty Cody." They were the parents of jazz guitar virtuoso Lenny Breau. Prior to the mid-1960s, country music was neither a homogenized genre nor dominated by the "Nashville Sound." There were regional styles of music. From the late 1940s through the early 1950s, Hal Lone Pine, Betty Cody, and the Lone Pine Mountaineers dominated the country music charts in Maine. In 1953, they became regulars on the *Wheeling Jamboree.* They also appeared on national television in Canada. The couple divorced, and Hal eventually returned to Maine. Hal and Betty were inducted into the Maine Country Music Association Hall of Fame in 1978 and 1979, respectively.

UNCLE LEM. This postcard of Uncle Lem shows a young guitar player named Johnny Smith (sitting second from the right). Smith (1922–2013) was born in Birmingham, Alabama. His family moved to Portland, Maine, when Johnny was a young boy. He joined Uncle Lem and His Mountain Boys, a local hillbilly band that travelled around Maine performing at fairs and dances. Smith earned $4 a night and quit high school to pursue a music career. He left Uncle Lem and His Mountain Boys at 18. Johnny Smith went on to become a legendary jazz guitar player.

KEN MACKENZIE. Ken MacKenzie (1918–1993) was born on Cape Breton Island, Nova Scotia, Canada. He started playing guitar in high school. In 1935, Ken auditioned and won a spot on WFEA in Manchester, New Hampshire. By 1938, he appeared on radio six days a week. That same year, he married his wife, Simone, who also performed with the band. In 1939, Ken moved to WGAN in Portland, Maine. He formed a variety show that included three pairs of female dancers. The group toured Maine, New Hampshire, and the Canadian Maritime Provinces. Ken started a weekly television show in 1954 that aired through 1971, when he retired. Simone and Ken were master yodelers. He was inducted into the Maine Country Music Association Hall of Fame (1978). In addition, Ken and Simone are members of the Yodeling Hall of Fame.

NORTHERN RIDGERUNNERS. This 1942 postcard shows the Northern Ridgerunners. They performed on WDEV from Waterbury, Vermont, and WWSR from St. Albans, Vermont.

DUKE AND HIS SWINGBILLIES. Michael J. "Duke" Pelillo (1916–1998) was born in Graniteville, Vermont. By 1939, Duke and His Swingbillies were performing on WHEB in Portsmouth, New Hampshire. Duke served with the US Army in France and Germany during World War II. This photograph was probably taken around 1946, when the group appeared on WMUR in Manchester, New Hampshire. Duke is pictured in the center of the back row.

AL RAWLEY AND THE WILD AZALEAS. Elton "Al" Rawley Jr. (1918–1999) was born in Boston, Massachusetts. About 1931, Al joined a group called the Rustlers. During World War II, several group members went into military service. This photograph shows the remaining members. From left to right are Elton Madison "Al" Rawley, Ray "Snuffy" Polo, and Paul "Shorty" Cyr, pictured at WEEI in Boston, Massachusetts. The group was renamed the Wild Azaleas. Al was elected to the Massachusetts Country Music Association Hall of Fame (1989).

COWBOY JACK. "Cowboy" Jack Henderson Clement (1931–2013) was a regular performer on the WCOP *Hayloft Jamboree* in Boston, Massachusetts. He became one of the most successful country music songwriters. His 10 number-one songs included "Ballad of a Teenage Queen," "Guess Things Happen That Way," "Just a Girl I Used to Know," "Not What I Had in Mind," and "Miller's Cave." He was inducted into the Nashville Songwriters Hall of Fame (1973), Music City Walk of Fame (2009), Rockabilly Hall of Fame (2011), Country Music Hall of Fame (2013), and Memphis Hall of Fame (2017).

GEORGE AND DIXIE. George and Dixie appeared on WNAC in Boston, Massachusetts, from about 1939 until April 1951. They regularly performed at their Pinecrest Ranch near Nasonville, Rhode Island. Although known as the Yodeling Twins, George and Dixie were neither twins nor relatives. They are members of the Massachusetts Country Music Association Hall of Fame (1992).

JERRY AND SKY. Jerry Howarth and Schuyler "Sky" Snow came from Portsmouth, New Hampshire. Their radio career began about 1938 and continued until the mid-1950s. Jerry and Sky could be heard over WHDH in Boston, Massachusetts, in 1944. They recorded for Sonora (1945), Decca (1949), and MGM. They performed with their band, the Melodymen, and are often credited with bringing bluegrass music to New England. They were inducted into the Massachusetts Country Music Association Hall of Fame (1985).

JIMMIE AND DICK. Pictured at left with his guitar, "Jimmie" Dana Marvin Pierson (1910–1996) was born in Kansas. On the right, playing accordion, Richard Benjamin "Noodle Soup" Klasi (1910–1981) was native to Utica, South Dakota. The boys met while working at the Henry Field Company in Norfolk, Nebraska. The company sponsored remote radio broadcasts from its store. Jimmie and Dick began singing and playing on the company shows. By 1934, they appeared on KMOX in St. Louis, Missouri. In 1937, they moved to WEEI in Boston, Massachusetts. By 1946, the Novelty Boys were working at WABI in Bangor, Maine. They were elected to America's Old Time Country Music Hall of Fame (2003).

TONY, JUANITA, AND BUDDY. This postcard of Buddy (left, fiddle), Juanita Labanara (guitar, 1915–1978), and Tony Tarquinio (guitar) was postmarked 1946. They were popular New England performers during the 1940s. Tony and Juanita were elected to the Maine Country Music Association Hall of Fame (1981).

THE BRONCHO BUSTERS. This photograph shows, from left to right, Cliff Japhet (mandolin), Elwin "Blondy" Harris (piano), Melvin "Mel" Nellis (guitar), Allen "Putch" Morley (banjo), and Lyman "Lym" Mead (violin). Cliff Japhet (1909–2007) was the cofounder of the Broncho Busters. They appeared on radio stations throughout Upstate New York and performed with noted celebrities such as Vernon Dalhart, the "Grandfather of Country Music." Japhet wrote or cowrote more than 1,000 songs. About 1945, he formed Cliff Japhet and the Western Aces. The Broncho Busters appeared in several Western movies, including *Galloping Thunder*.

DUSTY MILLER AND HIS COLORADO WRANGLERS. Elmer J. Rossi (1910–1997), also known as "Dusty Miller," was born and lived his entire life in Amsterdam, New York. He formed Dusty Miller and His Colorado Wranglers around 1932. His career continued into the 1990s. This postcard is postmarked Waterbury, Vermont (1941), and was probably taken when Dusty was appearing on WCAX in Burlington, Vermont. However, he spent most of his career broadcasting in his hometown on WCSS. According to a Bob Cudmore podcast, Dusty was a "radio legend" who was buried "in his beautiful cowboy clothes."

God Luck Pal – I'm yodelin' for you Olivio

OLIVIO SANTORO. Olivio Santoro (born 1928) was known as the "Boy Yodeler" and hosted his own syndicated radio show in New York City from the late 1930s to the early 1940s. He wrote the booklet "How to Yodel." Santoro wrote that "Yodeling is fun! Long before people knew any words, they expressed their happiness by yodeling. When you're happy, yodel! When you're sad, yodel and get happy. Come on, everybody . . . yodel along with me!" When World War II began, there was an increased sense of insecurity and paranoia in the United States. Olivio's show was cancelled because some people suspected that he might be communicating with Nazi sympathizers by yodeling. Olivio's career abruptly ended, and he drifted into obscurity.

Tony and his Lehigh Valley Boys

TONY AND HIS LEHIGH VALLEY BOYS. Tony and his Lehigh Valley Boys are pictured playing for WILM on August 20, 1944, in Wilmington, Delaware.

HAPPY JOHNNY AND HANDSOME BOB. "Happy Johnny" Zufall (guitar) and "Handsome Bob" Bouch (fiddle) performed on the *Wheeling Original Jamboree* in 1935 and on WORK (now named WOYK) York, Pennsylvania, during the 1940s. The *York Daily Record* reported, "During a silly song, Bob would roll his eyes and snap his suspenders and roll back and forth on his feet. He wore trousers that were two sizes too big and rolled the legs up above his socks."

THE 101 RANCH BOYS. "The 101 Ranch Boys Sponsored by the York Furniture Center appear 8:30 A.M. Daily 3:30 P.M. over WSBA & WSBA-FM. Thanks for listening!" The group included Leonard Zinn (steel guitar), George Long (fiddle), Andy Reynolds (guitar), Smokey Roberts (guitar), and Clifford Brown (fiddle). WSBA broadcast from York, Pennsylvania.

101 Ranch Boys Pennant. The group's name was suggested by Clifford Brown's mother. She was a Cherokee Indian who was raised on the 101 Ranch in Oklahoma. The band was formed in Kansas City, Kansas, during the 1930s and based in York, Pennsylvania. They recorded for Security, Rich, and Columbia Records. The 101 Ranch Boys performed with artists such as Gene Autry, Rex Allen, Ken Maynard, Jimmy Wakely, and Ken Curtis. They also performed for Pres. Harry S. Truman. The group remained active until around 1955.

Season's Greetings, LOG CABIN BOYS, W.O.R.K., York, Pa.

The Log Cabin Boys. This season's greetings postcard was sent to WORK listeners in 1946 from the Log Cabin Boys. WORK was a station in York, Pennsylvania. There are references to Frankie More's Log Cabin Boys appearing on the WWVA Wheeling Jamboree (1936). However, it is unknown if this postcard is a photo of the same group.

BLUE RIDGE MOUNTAINEERS. The Blue Ridge Mountaineers played out of Fleetwood, Pennsylvania. This state was the birthplace and home for many early country music groups. The Blue Ridge Mountaineers were a colorful act, which included fancy costumes and instruments as well as comedians with painted faces.

HILLSDALE HILLBILLIES. The Hillsdale Hillbillies included Bud Moore (banjo), Bill Jenkins (accordion), Cal Aughenbaugh (bass), and Grant "Zeke" Ogden (fiddle); they are pictured in this postcard dated 1941. Edgar A. "Bud" Moore (1918–2010) was born in Hillsdale, a small village near Clearfield, Pennsylvania. He started playing for square dances in 1929. Bud organized the Hillsdale Hillbillies in 1935. They won a talent contest in 1941 to become the first band to perform on WCED in DuBois, Pennsylvania, and on WCPA in Clearfield. During the 1950s, he had his own music show on WFBG-TV in Altoona, Pennsylvania. Bud Moore and the Hillsdale Hillbillies broadcast over 1,000 radio shows and entertained audiences for more than 75 years. Legendary fiddle player Buddy Spicher made his first stage appearance with the Hillsdale Hillbillies.

NORTH CAROLINA RIDGE RUNNERS. This photograph shows, from left to right, Johnie Miller, Arthur "Shorty" Wood, Ginger, Nick, and Bill. The North Carolina Ridge Runners were not based in that state, but several members moved from Ashe County, North Carolina, during the 1920s and 1930s. They performed on radio stations in Pennsylvania, West Virginia, Virginia, and Delaware. The original group included Ola Belle Campbell, who played banjo, guitar, and fiddle. Her brother Alex also played for the Ridge Runners. The group disbanded in 1948.

THE SOUTH MOUNTAIN RANGERS. The South Mountain Rangers broadcast over WFMD in Frederick, Maryland, and WCHS in Charleston, West Virginia. The back side of this postcard indicates that the group was performing at York Springs, Pennsylvania, on July 27, 1944. Admission was 15¢.

Hal Burns' Varieties

EB   JACKIE   LILLIE BELLE   GARLAND   TILLIE   UNCLE NED   JOHNNY   LONNIE

HAL AND SISSIE

HAL BURN'S VARIETIES. The Hal Burns Varieties appeared on WBRC-TV in Birmingham, Alabama, during the 1950s. Hal "Happy" Burns (1906–2000) was born in Mule Shoe, Texas. Burns began his radio career on WBRC Radio in the 1930s. He was one of the original movie cowboys and made a few Western films even before Gene Autry and Roy Rogers. Burns drove to concerts in his 1961 Pontiac Bonneville convertible that was a gift from Webb Pierce. The vehicle was decorated with 1,000 pounds of silver, including 250 silver dollars and 13 silver-plated pistols that replaced door handles and levers.

BLUE SEAL PALS AND POSTER. In 1943, the Blue Seal Pals were founded by Edgar Clayton (born 1923) and Quinton M. Clauch (born 1921). The photograph shows, from left to right, Dexter Johnson (bass), Bill Cantrell (fiddle), Edgar Clayton (guitar), and Quinton Clauch (guitar). Clauch was also a comic known as "Washboard." The Blue Seal Pals originally performed on radio station WLAY in Muscle Shoals, Alabama, and moved to Florence, Alabama, in 1946. The group later hosted *The Sun-Up Serenade* on WSM in Nashville, Tennessee. The Blue Seal Pals disbanded in 1948 when recorded music began to replace live radio shows.

CLYDE BAUM AND HIS HAPPY HILLBILLYS. Clyde Carl Baum (1917–1981) was born in Pollock, Louisiana. Clyde Baum and His Happy Hillbillys appeared on ABC KALB in Alexandria, Louisiana. He also performed on the *Louisiana Hayride*. Baum played mandolin on Hank Williams's first number-one hit, "Lovesick Blues."

HOOSIER CORNHUSKERS. The Hoosier Cornhuskers appeared on WFIN in Findley, Ohio, during the mid- to late 1940s. The band members consisted of, from left to right, LaVera Schaberow (bass), Clair L. Meekins (guitar), Pete "Grandpap" Smith (fiddle), Al Pettit (accordion), and Margaret Schaberow (guitar).

THE GEORGIA CRACKERS

OHIO STATE FAIR-1946

THE GEORGIA CRACKERS. This photograph of the Georgia Crackers was taken at the Ohio State Fair in 1946. Although the Newman brothers were born in Cochran, Georgia, they spent most of their career in the Midwest. They were the longest-performing act on WHKC in Columbus, Ohio. The Georgia Crackers, sometimes known as the Newman Brothers, consisted of Henry J. "Hank" Newman (1905–1978), Marion Alonzo "Slim" Newman (1910–1982), and Robert "Bob" Newman (1915–1979). Their singing style was similar to the Sons of the Pioneers. Winnie Waters (fiddle) and Hal Snyder (guitar) joined the brothers after their move to Columbus. After World War II, the group spent time in California, where it appeared in several of Charles Starrett's Durango Kid movies. It also established The G Bar C Ranch, a country music park near Columbus, Ohio.

MISSOURI FOX HUNTERS. From left to right are Jay, Happy, Shorty, and Marty Licklider. Martin Ellis "Marty" Licklider (1912–1994) was born in Jake Prairie, Missouri. His first radio job was with WTAM in Cleveland, Ohio. Marty then moved to Ashtabula, Ohio, where he formed the Missouri Fox Hunters. The group appeared on WICA from about 1938 to 1952. In 1952, he began performing on television over WICU in Erie, Pennsylvania.

JOE AND BILLY FOLGER. Joe and Billy Folger were featured on the KSTP *Barn Dance* and the *Sunrise Roundup* in Minneapolis, Minnesota. The KTSP *Sunset Valley Barn Dance* started on radio in 1940, eventually moved to television, and stayed on the air into the 1950s. The program's goal was to bring to listeners young and old alike "true American folk music, in its original form."

JOE   BILLY

Greetings from . . .

Joe and Billy Folger

Featured on the KSTP Barn Dance
And "The Sunrise Roundup"

Here's that picture you asked for, along with the words to Billy
Folger's new song hit which you'll find on the reverse side.
Thanks for listening . . . and thanks for writing in.

OZARK MOUNTAINEERS. Pictured here are the Ozark Mountaineers on KMOX in St. Louis, Missouri. The Ozark Mountaineers also appeared on the KWKH *Louisiana Hayride* and KWEM in Memphis, Tennessee.

JERRY SMITH AND ZELDA SCOTT. Jerry Smith and Zelda Scott, "Sweethearts of the Golden West," appeared on the WHO *Barn Dance Frolic* in Des Moines, Iowa, in 1942. Born in 1921, Zelda first performed at the WHO Iowa county fairs at age seven. She dropped out of high school and joined Jerry Smith on the *Iowa Barn Dance Frolic*. In 1946, their first recording, "Have I Told You Lately That I Love You" was issued on the Blue Star label.

TOM OWEN AND HIS COWBOYS. Tom Owen and His Cowboys were on WMT in Cedar Rapids, Iowa in 1938. The back of this postcard reads, "Greetings from Sheriff Tom Owen and His Cowboys featured over Radio Station WMT Cedar Rapids, Every Day at 11:15. We hope to meet you in person soon at your Favorite Dance Hall, Sincerely Yours, Tom Owen."

BOB AND JIM RAINES COMPLIMENTS NEBRASKA IGA STORES. Bob and Jim Raines were a father-and-son group. Bob picked old-time banjo around Fairmont, West Virginia, and his son Jim played guitar. During the 1940s, they published two hymnals, *Blue Ridge Mountain Hymnal* and *Bob and Jim's Radio Favorites No. 2*. They performed on several radio stations around the country, including stations in Lincoln, Nebraska.

MONTANA STEVE AND HIS SADDLE PALS.
This postcard shows a studio photo of
Montana Steve, with his name emblazoned
on his guitar, and His Saddle Pals from the
1940s. The boys are wearing fancy Western
outfits and hand-tooled leather boots to
go with their fiddle and guitars. While
the entire country seemed to embrace the
singing cowboy Western films, Montana
Steve and His Saddle Pals were a part
of the craze of the 1930s and 1940s.

KENNY ANDERSON, THE SINGING COWBOY—BILLINGS, MONT.   E-278

KENNY ANDERSON. Kenny Anderson, "the
Singing Cowboy," performed on KPOW
in Powell, Wyoming, in 1948, as well as in
Billings, Montana, where he appeared with
sponsorship from the Yellowstone County
Trades and Labor Assembly, Affiliated
with American Federation of Labor. They
noted that "Kenny will be very glad to hear
from you and sing your favorite Western
song." The November 27, 1948, edition of
Billboard reported that "Kenny Anderson,
'the Singing Cowboy,' is being aired over the
20 station Intermountain network. Show
emanates from KPOW, Powell, Wyo."

THE OKLAHOMA TRAVELERS. The name Oklahoma Travelers has been used many times. However, the Wright Bros. remain as unknown performers.

JACK PERRY AND THE LIGHT CRUST DOUGHBOYS. Pictured around 1946, Jack Perry and the Light Crust Doughboys are, from left to right (first row) Mel Cox a.k.a. "Jack Perry, (fiddle and announcer), John "Knocky" Parker (accordion), J.R. "Sleepy" Kidwell (bass), and Fred "Ezra" Casares (fiddle); (second row) Jake "Curly" Wright (guitar), Dick "Junior" Dyson (banjo), Wilson "Lefty" Perking (guitar), and Clifford Gross (fiddle). The Light Crust Doughboys were a Western swing band formed in 1931 by the Burris Grain and Elevator Company in Saginaw, Texas. The group achieved continued success until World War II, when its radio show was cancelled. In 1946, Burris Grain attempted to launch a new program with Jack Perry. The five-string banjo player from Columbus, Indiana, was leader of the group until 1948. The Light Crust Doughboys are members of the Texas Cowboy, Texas Swing, Rockabilly, Texas Music, Texas Radio, and Cowtown Society of Western Music Halls of Fame.

Texas Jim Lewis. "Texas" Jim Lewis (1909–1990) was born in Meigs, Georgia. From 1932 to 1934, he played with the Swift Jewel Cowboys in Houston. Lewis then formed the Lone Star Cowboys, which included his half-brother Jack Rivers and Smokey Rogers. They moved to New York City, where they performed regularly at the Village Barn. The group recorded 40 sides for Decca Records. Lewis appeared in 42 Western films. In 1950, he moved to Seattle and established his Rainier Ranch. For seven years, Texas Jim hosted a popular children's TV show, *Sheriff Tex's Safety Junction*.

BILL LONG and THE RANCH GIRLS
EXCLUSIVE LONDON RECORDING ARTISTS

Bill Long and the Ranch Girls. Bill Long was born near Albuquerque, New Mexico, on his family's 2,000-acre ranch. By the age of 10, Bill would sit on the corral, sing, and play guitar. When he was 18, Bill joined the rodeo circuit in the United States and Canada. When one of his friends was seriously injured in a chuck wagon race, Bill decided to abandon rodeo to pursue a music career. In 1942, he was offered his first radio job on KMOX in St. Louis, Missouri. He soon moved to WHAS in Louisville, Kentucky, and then the *National Barn Dance*. After his days in Chicago, Bill met Madeline Bonin (who played bass and fiddle) and Dorothy Miller (who played steel guitar). They became known as Bill Long and the Ranch Girls. While touring Canada, they signed a recording contract with London Records. They were one of the first American acts to guest star and become regular cast members of the CMHL *Main Street Jamboree* in Hamilton, Ontario.

DIAMOND CREEK RAMBLERS. The Diamond Creek Ramblers were from Silver City, New Mexico.

ELSIE ANDERSON AND HER WESTERNERS. Elsie Anderson and Her Westerners broadcast over KTYL, as well as KRIZ in Phoenix, Arizona. An advertisement in the *Arizona Republic* dated December 13, 1947, stated that radio entertainers Elsie Anderson and Her Westerners were performing at the Seven Seas Club on Broadway at Central Avenue with dancing on Friday and Saturday nights. On November 7, 1953, the same newspaper advertised that "Every Wed.-Fri.-Sat.-Sun. Elsie Anderson and Her Westerners Now Playing at Diamond Tavern 4029 East Washington Street."

SLIM AND CLYDE. This is a postcard of Slim and Clyde performing on KFPY in Spokane, Washington in 1941. Slim and Clyde were a guitar and mandolin duo from Washington.

A Merry Christmas and a Happy New Year ——

THE SNEED FAMILY. Around 1952, the Sneed Family began performing in the Spokane, Washington, area. The group included Don Sneed (guitar) and his three sons, Leslie (mandolin), Don Jr. (accordion), and Danny (steel guitar). They appeared on television and performed throughout the Pacific Northwest and Canada. They recorded for Cascade Records.

"THE SNEED FAMILY"
Stars of Stage, Radio, TV and Cascade Recordings
2815 West 9th Avenue, Spokane, Washington

Five

NEARLY FORGOTTEN COUNTRY MUSIC PERFORMERS

JOHN WHITE. John I. White (1902–1992) was born in Washington, DC. In 1926, he became the first person to perform cowboy songs on a national radio program. White remained a popular entertainer and recording artist through the 1930s. He worked by different stage names, including the "Lone Star Ranger" and the "Lonesome Cowboy." His most memorable recordings were "Get Along Little Dogies" and "Strawberry Roan." John retired in 1965 and spent his remaining years researching Western music and the composers of cowboy songs.

BEST WISHES FROM DOC. SCHNEIDER'S TEXANS

Doc Schneider and His Texans. This postcard features Doc Schneider's Texans at Radio City Music Hall in New York City. An online article in *Between the Covers Books* included a photo album entitled "Doc Schneider's Texas Yodeling Cowboys and Ford Rangers" by Whit Gorusch, who was known as the "Wizard of the Banjo and Guitar." Whit was a member of Doc's group, which became a house band on the 500,000-watt Mexican border station XER and broadcast on NBC during the 1930s.

JANE SHANNON AND HER NITE HERDERS. Pictured are Jane Shannon and Her Nite Herders.

SHORTY SUTTON AND HIS FAMILY. This postcard shows Shorty Sutton and His Family in Shirley, Indiana.

JIMMY BOYD. Jimmy Devon Boyd (1939–2009) was born in McComb, Mississippi. His father was a struggling cotton farmer. In 1941, his father purchased train tickets to Riverside, California, for Jimmy, his mother, and a brother. The father did not have money for another ticket but joined them as a stowaway on a freight train. The family eventually grew to 21 children. At the age of seven, Jimmy and his family attended a barn dance in Colton, California. At the suggestion of a brother, Jimmy was asked to come on stage and sing. He soon became a regular performer on Texas Jim Lewis's radio show. Boyd went on to win a KLAC-TV talent show in Los Angeles, which led to other television appearances. In 1952, Jimmy recorded "I Saw Mommy Kissing Santa Claus." The song became number one on the charts and soon sold a reported two and half million copies. Jimmy went on to make other successful records, including duets with Frankie Laine and Rosemary Clooney. He also appeared on television programs such as the *Frank Sinatra Show, Betty White Show,* and *Bachelor Father.* Boyd's movie credits included his roles as a biology student in *Inherit the Wind* with Spencer Tracy and *High Times* with Bing Crosby.

Six

GOSPEL MUSIC GROUPS

THE ADDELSBERGER FAMILY, IN HIS SERVICE, WAYNESBORO, PA, R.D.2. Gospel music has always been an important part of country and western music. Tennessee Ernie Ford and Red Foley ended their television programs with a song of faith and inspiration. Most traditional country artists recorded gospel selections. The Brown's Ferry Four was a legendary gospel group that included Alton Denmore, Rabon Delmore, Grandpa Jones, and Merle Travis, who was later replaced by Red Foley. Albert E. Brumley was perhaps the greatest American gospel songwriter (including "I'll Fly Away" and "Turn Your Radio On").

THE FAVORITE MELODY QUARTET. The Favorite Melody Quartet, from Knoxville, Tennessee, was, from left to right, Bessie, Ernest, Oma, Hurstle, and J.R. Whitlock. The group was widely known as the Wheel Chair Singers and performed gospel music.

RALPH OVERLY'S GOSPEL QUARTETTE. This photograph shows Ralph Overly's Gospel Quartette.

THE GOSPEL MESSENGERS. The Gospel Messengers are photographed with banners reading "He Died for You" and "Praise Ye the Lord." They used xylophones, saxophones, guitars, and an accordion to deliver their spiritual message.

MARTHA CARSON. Irene Amburgey (1921–2004), later known as Martha Carson, was born in Neon, Kentucky. The singer and songwriter was known as the "Rockin' Queen of Happy Gospel." In grammar school, Martha began playing folk songs and spirituals on her mail-order guitar. She was writing songs before she was 10. In 1936, Martha and her sisters, Bertha and Opal, formed the Sunshine Sisters. She appeared on the *Renfro Valley Barn Dance* and became a member of the Coon Creek Girls. In 1938, the Amburguey sisters (nicknamed Minnie, Marthie, and Mattie) were invited to join the WSB *Barn Dance* in Atlanta. In 1940, she teamed up with her mandolin player husband, James Carson Roberts as the Barn Dance Sweethearts. In 1950, they divorced, and Martha began making solo appearances. In 1951, she made her recording of "Satisfied," a gospel song written in response to audience disapproval of her divorce. From 1952 to 1957, she was a member of the *Grand Ole Opry*. She then married Xavier Crosse, moved to New York City, and started a family.

MARTHA CARSON'S SPIRITUAL SONG FOLIO NO. 1, 1954. During the early 1950s, Carson toured with Ferlin Husky, Jimmy Dickens, Moon Mullican, and Elvis Presley. After their performances, Elvis and Martha would sing gospel songs. Presley stated that Martha had more influence on his stage style that any other individual. Carson was inducted into the Atlanta Country Music Hall of Fame (1985).

THE SULLIVAN FAMILY. This photograph of the Sullivan Family was taken during the early 1960s. Enoch Hugh Sullivan (1931–2011) was born in the Tombigbee Valley area of southern Alabama. His wife, Margie, was born in 1933 in Winnsboro, Louisiana. In 1948, the Sullivan Family began performing on radio in Jackson, Alabama. They were known as a hard-driving bluegrass gospel group and performed from about 1949 to 1999. Bill Monroe referred to them as "The First Family of Bluegrass Gospel Music." They were inducted into Bill Monroe's Bluegrass Hall of Fame in Bean Blossom, Indiana, and the Old Time Country Music Hall of Fame. One of the Sullivan Family musicians was a 12-year old mandolin player named Marty Stuart. (Courtesy of Jonathan Causey.)

Seven

COUNTRY MUSIC ADVERTISEMENTS

GREETINGS FROM THE COTTON QUEEN CAST AND PERUNA. About 1890, a Columbus, Ohio, physician by the name of Samuel Brubaker Hartman invented a medicine he called Peruna. Dr. Hartman advertised that his tonic was a cure for "catarrh," which included asthma, pneumonia, tuberculosis, cancer, and virtually all known disease. It became the largest-selling proprietary medicine in the United States. Since Peruna had an alcohol content of 28 percent, it was banned from sale on Indian reservations and was known as "Prohibition tonic." Apparently, folks who listened to country music loved the medicinal kick of Peruna. From about 1935 to 1946, Peruna advertisements included a card with a calendar on one side and photographs of country music celebrities on the other. This one advertises from 1935, "Greetings from the Cotton Queen Cast and Peruna—WLW Cincinnati, Ohio—Try Peruna To Help Build Up Cold Chasing Cold Fighting Resistance."

WITH BEST WISHES FROM THE WHO BARN DANCE AND PERUNA. This advertisement was sent from the WHO *Barn Dance* of Des Moines, Iowa, in 1935.

GREETINGS FROM HAPPY HAL O'HALLORAN'S HOUSEWARMERS. Greetings from Happy Hal O'Halloran's Housewarmers, WOR in New York City, and Peruna, 1935. Harold James "Hal" O'Halloran was a radio announcer and singer. He was master of ceremonies for the *National Barn Dance* on WLS Chicago (1930–1934). He later became an announcer at WOR New York City in 1935, where he hosted *Hal O'Halloran's Housewarmers*.

CUMBERLAND RIDGE RUNNERS AND PERUNA. "With the Season's Compliments and Best Wishes from the Cumberland Ridge Runners and Peruna" at the WLS *National Barn Dance* in Chicago, Illinois. The Cumberland Ridge Runners were regular performers on the *National Barn Dance*. The group included Karl Davis (guitar), Hartford Taylor (mandolin), Hugh Cross (banjo and guitar), Homer Miller (fiddle), and Clyde "Red" Foley (bass and vocals).

THE WESTERNERS AND PERUNA. "Greetings from the Westerners and Peruna" at the WLS *National Barn Dance* in Chicago, Illinois, 1935. Louise Massey and the Westerners were a family group from New Mexico. They appeared on the *National Barn Dance* during the 1930s and 1940s. A listener in Iowa claimed to have kept track of how many songs the Westerners sang: 3,292 live songs and 501 recordings.

OZARK MOUNTAINEERS AND PERUNA. "Greetings from the Ozark Mountaineers," KMOX in St. Louis, Missouri, and Peruna, 1935. The St. Louis Media History Foundation reported that in 1932, Len Johnson and His Ozark Mountaineers "are on and off the stage playing real hillbilly tunes." The group also performed on the KWKH *Louisiana Hayride*.

UTAH BUCKAROOS, KSL, AND PERUNA. "Greetings from the Utah Buckaroos, KSL [in Salt Lake City, Utah,] and Peruna," 1935. The Utah Buckaroos did not leave a lasting legacy in radio or singing cowboy history. However, they are perhaps one of the only groups that featured a lasso to entertain and "rope in" their audience.

JULES ALLEN AND HIS COWHANDS AND PERUNA, 1935. Jules Allen (1883–1945) was born in Waxahachie, Texas. He was one the early radio singing cowboys and worked as a horse wrangler, ranch hand, and Texas Ranger. In 1933, he published a book entitled *Cowboy Lore* that provided a first-person account of the daily life of a working cowboy, including terms and sayings and a collection of "Songs on the Range."

KLRD, LONNIE AND HIS BOYS, AND PERUNA. "Greetings from KLRD Lonnie and His Boys from Sugar Creek and Peruna," 1935.

GREETINGS FROM "PAPPY" CHESIRE'S HILL BILLY BAND AND PERUNA

—"Ozark Melodeers"—

STANDING
(Left to Right)
AMBROSE HALEY (The Ozark Rambler)
ROY QUEEN (The Lone Singer)
FREDDIE EASTERDAY (The Mountain Shadow)
HARRY CAMPBELL (Dynamite Jim)
JOHNNY BUFFINGTON

HAZEL CAMPBELL
(Texas Bluebonnet)
HELEN GRAHAM
(Little Ozark Sweetheart)
LUCILE BENNETT
(Texas Bluebonnet)

—"Ozark Mountaineers"—
EDDIE GENTRY
CARL McDANIELS
"DIXIE BOY" AARON JORDON
"SHUCKS" EDDIE AUSTIN
"STUFFY" CHARLES AUSTIN

KNEELING (Left)
FRANKIE KRATCIR
"SKEETS" YANEY (The Golden-Voiced Yodeler)

SEATED (In Center)
BILL HOGLUND
DAVE PEARSON
ANDY ANDREASON

} "Three Hired Men"

KNEELING (Right)
JIMMIE PEARSON
DICK KLASI

} "The Novelty Boys"

"Pappy"

"PAPPY" CHESIRE'S HILL BILLY BAND AND PERUNA. Greetings from "Pappy" Chesire's Hill Billy Band and Peruna, 1936. The WHO *Barn Dance Frolic* (also known as the *Iowa Barn Dance Frolic*) was broadcast on WHO and later WHO-TV in Des Moines, Iowa. The show ran from 1931 until the 1950s.

PERUNA AND **WHO** BARN DANCE FROLIC. "Greetings from Peruna and WHO *Barn Dance Frolic*" in Des Moines, Iowa, 1936. By 1935, the program was expanded to a three-hour production and was moved to the Shrine Auditorium to accommodate a seating capacity of 4,200 attendees.

PANHANDLE RANGERS, WWVA, AND PERUNA. "Greetings from the Panhandle Rangers, WWVA" in Wheeling, West Virginia, and Peruna, 1936. The Peruna Panhandle Rangers appeared on the WWVA *Original Jamboree* in 1934. The group included Elmer Crone, who was known as "the Wandering Minstrel" and was one of the Jamboree's earliest performers. Other members included Fred Gardini, Blaine Heck, Paul Myers, and Dutch Haid.

PERUNA AND THE PRAIRIE RAMBLERS. Greetings from Peruna, the Prairie Ramblers—Jack Taylor, Tex Atchison, Salty Holmes, Chick Hurt, Joe Kelly, Patsy Montana, and "Henry Hornsbuckle"— and the WLS *National Barn Dance*, Chicago, Illinois, 1936. The Prairie Ramblers were classic *National Barn Dance* singing cowboys. They appeared in several Gene Autry and Rex Allen movies. Their final recording sessions were done for Mercury Records in late 1947.

113

CROCKETT FAMILY, KNX, AND PERUNA. Greetings from the Crockett Family, KNX in Los Angeles, and Peruna, 1936. The Crocket Family was formed by John Harvey "Dad" Crockett and included George (fiddle), Johnny (banjo, guitar, and vocals), Alan (fiddle and bones), Clarence (guitar), and Albert (tenor guitar). The group recorded in Los Angeles and New York (1928–1931) and disbanded in 1938. Alan later replaced Tex Atchison on fiddle in the Prairie Ramblers.

THE RANCH HOUSE GANG—Left to right: Bob Howell, Little Peggy, Mother Leary, Slippery Slim, Your Peruna Announcer "Dutch" Woodward, Wilma Lee, Jessie Mae, Cowboy Ben, and Miss Jerry.

Left to right, standing: Hugh Aspinwell, Red Phillips, Dolly Good, Grandpa Jones, Happy Hal O'Halloran. Left to right, seated: Texas Ruby, Pa and Ma McCormick, Curly Fox.

Asher Sizemore and Little Jimmie

THE RANCH HOUSE GANG. The Ranch House Gang in 1943 is, from left to right, (first row) Texas Ruby, Pa and Ma McCormich, and Curly Fox; (second row) Hugh Aspinwell, Red Phillips, Dolly Good, Grandpa Jones, and Happy O'Halloran. For more than 20 years, Clarence "Pa" McCormick (1872–1945) and Alice "Ma" McCormick (1874–1958) were the patriarch and matriarch of WLW Cincinnati, Ohio. They were also featured on the *Top o' the Morning Show* and *Boone County Jamboree*. Pa and Ma were from northern Kentucky and played harmonica and piano, respectively.

EARLY MORNING FROLIC. Early Morning Frolic, pictured in 1943, is, from left to right, (first row) Jack Holden and Fairly Holden (second row) Molly O'Day, Lynn Davis, Randy Barnett, and Lonnie Glosson. The Pony Express Round Up Gang is, from left to right, (first row) Minor Clites and his seeing-eye dog Joy, Virginia Drowns, and Mae and Oma West; (second row) Tommy Davis, Ray Murrell, Harry Packard, Carlton Schirmer, and Bunkhouse Bill. At bottom are, from left to right, (first row) Curley; (second row) Helen, Margaret, Zeke, Herbie, M.C., Steve, Pauline, Ted Cook, Nadine, and Elmer; (third row) Bill Piney, Sleepy, and Roy.

EARLY MORNING FROLIC—Left to right (rear): Molly O'Day, Lynn Davis, Randy Barnett, Lonnie Glosson. Left to right (seated): Jack Holden and Fairly Holden.

THE PONY EXPRESS ROUND-UP GANG—Standing, left to right: Tommy Davis, Ray Murrell, Harry Packard, Carlton Schirmer, Bunkhouse Bill. Sitting, left to right: Minor Clites, Virginia Drowns, The West Sisters (Mae and Oma) and Minor Clites' Seeing Eye Dog—Joy.

Back Row: Bill (Piney), Sleepy, Roy. Standing: Helen, Margaret, Zeke, Herbie, M. C., Steve, Pauline, Ted Cook, Nadine, Elmer. Seated: Curley.

Left to right: First step, Cousin Emmy and Johnny Creasy; second step Bill Drake and Hal Choisser; third step, "Little Shoe" Wade Ray and Molly Lou; standing, Jack Drake, Sid Saunders, program announcer, Pappy Cheshire, master of ceremonies, and Chuck Davis.

Front row: Clyde Moffett, Doc Hopkins, Jack Stilwill, Ozzie Westley, Patsy Montana and Harry Simms. Back row: Karl Davis, Reuben Raymond, Augie Klein, "Ding" Bell and Harty Taylor.

Asher Sizemore and Little Jimmie

COUSIN EMMY AND JOHNNY CREASY. From left to right in 1943 are (first row) Cousin Emmy and Johnny Creasy; (second row) Bill Drake and Hal Choisser; (third row) "Little Shoe" Wade Ray and Molly Lou; (fourth row) Jack Drake; Sid Saunders, program announcer; Pappy Cheshire, master of ceremonies; and Chuck Davis. Below are, from left to right, (first row) Clyde Moffett, Doc Hopkins, Jack Stilwill, Ozzie Westley, Patsy Montana, and Harry Simms; (second row) Karl Davis, Reuben Raymond, Augie Klein, "Ding" Bell, and Hank Taylor. At bottom are Asher Sizemore and Little Jimmie Peruna advertises itself as "The famous tonic that helps to win fights with colds by helping to build up resistance, such resistance often preventing and relieving colds."

NEW PERUNA. "Compliments and Wishes from the New Peruna." From left to right are (top) Kaktus Kids, Uncle Enoch and His Gang, Pete Haley and His Log Cabin Girls, and the Bohemian Orchestra; (middle) Cousin Emmy and Her Gang, the Briarhoppers, the Haden Family, and the Bar Nothing Gang; (bottom) Cap, Andy, Milt, Charlie and Honey, and Orville Miller; the Smiling Hillbillies; and Morning Frolic. Beginning in 1930, Samuel Warren "Cap" Caplinger (1889–1957) on guitar, Andrew "Andy" Patterson (1893–1950) on fiddle, and William Austin "Flip" Strickland (1908–1988) on banjo and mandolin enjoyed a successful radio career on WWVA *Original Jamboree* and other stations. The repertoire consisted primarily of gospel songs. Around 1940, Flip's son Milt joined the trio. In 1949, the group disbanded due to Andy's poor health.

LAFE HARKNESS, CHESTER ATKINS. From left to right are (top) Lafe Harkness, Chester Atkins, the Callahan Brothers, Ben and Jessie Mae Norma, the Blue Bonnet Girls, and Pete Cassel, "King of the Hillbillies"; (middle) Little Joe's Jamboree, and the Sons of the Pioneers; (bottom) the Turner Brothers, Guy Blakeman, Will Lenay, and the Herrington Sisters. In this 1946 ad, Zymole Trokeys claims to provide "Fast, Quick Relief for Coughs Due to Colds, Smokers' Throat, Huskiness and Similar Throat Irritations." The product is no longer manufactured, and the patent expired about 1988.

SUMMERTIME FROLICS FOLKS. Greetings from the Summertime Frolics Folks in 1940. From left to right are(seated) Jackie Davis and Uncle Ervin Victor; (standing) Harty Taylor, Shelby Jean Davis (also known as "Little Mountain Sweetheart"), Karl Davis, Billy Flannery, Doc Hopkins, Betty Casper, Mert Minnick, and Ginny Casper.

WLW, CINCINNATI. An advertisement for Zymole Trokeys features artists on WLW Radio in Cincinnati in 1940. At left is Tex Owens, the "Original Texas Ranger." At center are Pa and Ma McCormick, the "Dad and Mother of the Top of the Morning Gang." On the right, are Millie and Dollie, the "Girls of the Golden West." Tex Owens (1892–1962) was a singer and songwriter best known for his composition of the Eddy Arnold hit "Cattle Call." He was posthumously inducted into the Nashville Songwriters Hall of Fame in 1971.

WHAS Kentucky Play Party, Louisville. This 1940 ad sends "Greetings from WHAS *Kentucky Play Party*." From left to right are (first row) Gordon Sizemore, Little Betty, Johnny Ford, and Chuckwagon Joe; (second row) Sunshine Sue, Howard Sizemore, Mrs. Sizemore, Mary Lou, Uncle Henry, Pauline, and Randy Blake; (third row) George and Sam Workman, Randall Atcher, John Workman, Curly Bradshaw, Doc and Carl, and Rufus and Sally; (fourth row) Accordion Al, Coonhunter, Jim Shea, Barn Dancer, and Hilly Foy; (fifth row) Wanda Sizemore and Barn Dancers.

"Greetings from the Morning Jamboree." WHAS sent this ad in 1941. From left to right are (first row) Ray Cook, Joe and Bess—"Sweethearts of the Saddle"—and Casey Jones; (second row) Sally, Melvin Dupree, Curly Bradshaw, and Judy Lane; (third row) Uncle Henry, Bud Dumas, Hezzy Hall, Hilly Foy, "Toots," Les Cobb, Coonhunter, and Randy Blake. Sally and Coon Hunter sang older sentimental ballads. Curly Bradshaw played harmonica. Randy Blake (1906–1976) was emcee for the program.

COUSIN EMMY AND HER KINFOLK.
This 1942 advertising card includes photographs of Cousin Emmy and Her Kinfolk, Uncle Henry and His Kentucky Mountaineers, Asher and Little Jimmie, Patsy Montana and Little Beverly, the Carter Family and the Mainers, and Cowboy Slim Rinehart.

THE HERRINGTON SISTERS. This advertising card from 1947 includes photographs of the Herrington Sisters, the Callahan Brothers, Grandpa Jones, Hank Penny, Cowboy Copas, Bill Carlisle, the Delmore Brothers, and Hawkshaw Hawkins. The Herrington Sisters inncluded Ida Nell, Winnie, and Olga Herrington. They were a popular radio act on KWFT Wichita Falls, Texas, during the late 1940s and recorded for Mercury Records.

THE CARTER FAMILY (Above)
Top Row: A. P. Carter, Janette, Brother Bill, Sara, May-
belle. Children: Helen, Aneta and June.
MAINER'S MOUNTAINEERS (Right)
Standing: J. E. Mainer, Price "Grandpa". Seated: Ollie
and Zeke.

THE CARTER FAMILY. Stuart's Tablets offered relief from intense suffering due to "Frun Dyspepsia" and stomach trouble. The Carter Family is, from left to right, (first row) Helen, Anita, and June; (second row) A.P. Carter, Jeanette, Brother Bill, Sara, and Maybelle. The Mainer's Mountaineers are, from left to right, (first row) Ollie and Zeke; (second row) J.E. Mainer and Price "Grandpa." The official 1940 National League schedule, with the slogan "Stuart's Tablets Relieve Discomfort of Excess Stomach Acidity," is displayed diagonally across the back side of the card.

THE BLUE RIDGE MOUNTAIN BOYS
Jim and Bob Raines—KWTO

THE RURAL RAMBLERS—KFRU (Above)
Left to Right: Cowboy Bill Newcomb; Fiddlin' Sheriff; The Texas
Bluebonnet; Dynamite Jim; Sue; Sally; Jolly Dan; Handsome
Harry. At Table: Bill Haley.

THE RURAL RAMBLERS. The Rural Ramblers, appearing on KFRU, are, from left to right, Cowboy Bill Newcomb, Fiddlin' Sheriff, the Texas Bluebonnet, Dynamite Jim, Sue, Sally, Jolly, Dan, and Handsome Harry; Bill Haley is seated at the table. The Blue Ridge Mountain Boys, appearing on KWTO, are Jim and Bob Raines. The official 1940 American League schedule is displayed diagonally across the back of this card, again with the Stuart's Tablets slogan.

FOLEY'S HONEY & TAR SYRUP. Foley's Honey & Tar Syrup was bottled from the late 1800s to the mid-1960s. The product contained 7 percent alcohol and was used for clearing phlegm and mucus from the throat and clearing air passages for easier breathing.

THE DELMORE BROTHERS. This postcard features the Delmore Brothers and says: "Thank you for your letter! Here's your picture of Uncle Abner and the Delmore Brothers at the Cross Roads Store, and we know you'll like Duck Head overalls and work clothing just as much as you like their program! Now about the big prize! Every week we give $25 cash for the best rhyme about Duck Heads. All you have to do is enter a rhyme of not more than ten lines on why you like Duck Head overalls and mail it to us. Winner's name will be announced every Saturday night at 7:45 C.S.T. over WSM! Send yours today!" The Duck Head clothing brand was founded in 1865 in Nashville, Tennessee. The company became known as the O'Bryan Brothers Manufacturing Company.

ERNEST TUBB. This great advertising card shows Ernest Tubb (1914–1984) holding Jimmie Rodgers's guitar, a gift from Jimmie's widow. The musical presentation was sponsored by Universal Mills on KGKO 570 of Fort Worth, Texas. Ernest Tubb was born on a cotton farm near Crisp, Texas. He was a pioneer country music singer and songwriter, known as "The Texas Troubadour." His biggest hit record was "Walking the Floor Over You" (1941). He starred in the film *Hollywood Barn Dance* (1947). His lifetime achievements included the Hollywood Walk of Fame (1960), Country Music Hall of Fame (1965), Nashville Songwriters Hall of Fame (1970), Academy of Country Music Pioneer (1980), Music City News Living Legend Award (1984), and Texas Country Music Hall of Fame (1999).

Eight

THE FOLK SONG REVIVAL

ASH GROVE MENU. The folk song revival can be traced from the 1940s through the 1960s. College students and younger crowds listened to Woody Guthrie, Pete Seeger, the New Lost City Ramblers, and Folkway Records. Stringed instrument sales and lessons increased dramatically during this period. Folk music was performed at coffeehouses and festivals throughout America. Popular Southern California venues included the Troubadour (Santa Monica), Ash Grove (West Los Angeles) and Ice House (Pasadena). Beer and wine were not offered, but there was plenty of hot apple cider. Country music was energized during the folk song revival. The Dillards, Flatt and Scruggs, and the Stoneman Family were among country and folk music crossover acts of the era. UCLA Folk Festival performers included the Blue Sky Boys, Joe and Rose Lee Maphis, Merle Travis, and Doc Watson. This Ash Grove menu was signed by Merle Travis and Roger Miller in 1968. The Ash Grove (1958–1973) was a small folk music venue located at 6162 Melrose Avenue in Los Angeles.

The Original Dillards

Keith Case & Associates
1016 16th Ave. South
Nashville, Tennesse, 37212
(615) 255-1313

KSON PRESENTS:
IN CONCERT!
LESTER
FLATT &
EARL
SCRUGGS
ONE
BIG
SHOW
8 PM
SAT.
FEB.
11

RUSS AUDITORIUM   Tickets: $2.00 - $2.50 - $3.00

BUY YOUR TICKETS AT: Thearles, Downtown and Mission Valley;
House of Music, National City and Chula Vista; Valley Music,
El Cajon; KSON Radio, College Grove Center; All Naval Special
Services.

Presented by Station KSON, Country-Western Music, Dial 1240

THE DILLARDS. The Dillards, a bluegrass band from Salem, Missouri, are pictured in 1963. The original members shown in the photograph are, from left to right, Dean Webb (1937–2018) on mandolin, Mitchell Franklin "Mitch" Jayne (1929–2010) on bass, Douglas "Doug" Dillard (born 1937) on banjo, and Rodney Dillard (born 1942) on guitar. From 1963 to 1966, the group appeared as the Darling family on the *Andy Griffith Show*.

FLATT AND SCRUGGS. This program was signed by Lester Flatt and Earl Scruggs at a 1968 concert in San Diego. Lester Flatt (1914–1979) and Earl Scruggs (1924–2012) left Bill Monroe's Blue Grass Boys in 1948 and formed the Foggy Mountain Boys. They performed together until 1969. Flatt and Scruggs were inducted into the Country Music Hall of Fame (1985) and the Bluegrass Hall of Honor (1991).

THE STONEMAN FAMILY. This 1960s Stoneman Family photograph includes, from left to right, Veronica Loretta "Roni" Stoneman (born 1938) on banjo, Van Haden Stoneman (guitar, 1941–1995), Ernest Van "Pop" Stoneman (autoharp, 1893–1968), Oscar James "Jimmy" Stoneman (bass, 1937–2002), Donna Laverne Stoneman (mandolin, born 1934), and Jerry Monday (dobro). The Stoneman Family originated with Ernest V. "Pop" Stoneman, who was born in a log cabin in Carroll County, Virginia. Pop and his wife, Hattie, had 23 children, with 13 surviving to adulthood. In 1924, Pop made his first recordings for Okeh Records, including his million-seller "The Sinking of the Titanic." Between 1925 and 1934, he recorded more than 200 songs. In 1931, the family moved to Washington, DC, where Pop worked in a naval gun factory. After World War II, Pop gradually began their return to entertaining. The band members consisted of Hattie and several of their children. In 1956, Pop won a $10,000 prize on *The Big Surprise*, a television game show. Soon thereafter, the family won a talent contest on the *Arthur Godfrey Show*. In 1957, the Stoneman Family recorded for Folkways Records and embarked on a new career. The family became a popular folk music group. They moved to California, where they performed at the Monterey Folk Festival and on the coffeehouse circuit. In 1965, the Stoneman Family moved to Nashville and had a syndicated television show. In 1967, they made film appearances in *Hell on Wheels* and *Road to Nashville*. During that same year, they were voted Vocal Group of the Year by the Country Music Association. Pop was elected to the Autoharp Hall of Fame (1994) and Country Music Hall of Fame (2008).

Doc Watson. Arthel Lane "Doc" Watson (1923–2012) was born in Stoney Fork, North Carolina. As an infant, Doc developed an eye infection that resulted in blindness. As a six-year-old, he began playing harmonica. At 11, he started playing a fretless banjo made by his father. Two years later, Doc began playing guitar. He became a legendary flat-pick and finger-style guitar player. Watson was known for performing country, blues, folk, bluegrass, and gospel music. When Doc was about 18, he traveled "way across the mountain" to meet an old-time fiddler named Gaither Carlton. Six years later, he married Gaither's daughter Rosa Lee. In 1949, Rosa Lee gave birth to their son, Eddy Merle Watson (who was named after Eddy Arnold and Merle Travis). In 1961, Doc, Gaither Carlton, Tom Ashley, Fred Price, and Clint Howard traveled to New York City to perform at a folk music concert. They began performing regularly at coffeehouses throughout the country. Doc became widely acclaimed after his appearance at the Newport Folk Festival in 1963 and 1964. He performed with his son, Merle, from 1964 until Merle died in a 1985 tractor accident. In 1987, Doc began Merlefest at Wilkes Community College in Wilkesboro, North Carolina. This annual event remains one of the most popular and enduring bluegrass festivals in America. Doc received eight Grammy awards, including the Lifetime Achievement Award, and was inducted into the Bluegrass Hall of Honor (2000).

RECOMMENDED SITES

AllMusic. www.allmusic.com
America's Old Time Country Music Hall of Fame. www.music-savers.com/hall-of-fame
Bluegrass Music Association of Maine. www.mainebluegrass.org
Country Music Hall of Fame. countrymusichalloffame.org
Encyclopedia of Arkansas. encylopediaofarkansas.net
Grand Ole Opry. www.opry.com
Hillbilly-Music dawt com. www.Hillbilly-Music.com
The History of WLS Radio. www.wlshistory.com
International Bluegrass Music Association. ibma.org
Kentucky Music Hall of Fame. www.kentuckymusichalloffame.com
Nashville Songwriters Hall of Fame. nashvillesongwritersfoundation.com
National Fiddler Hall of Fame. nationalfiddlerhalloffame.org
Rockabilly Hall of Fame. www.rockabillyhall.com
Texas Country Music Hall of Fame & The Tex Ritter Museum. tcmhof.com
West Virginia Music Hall of Fame. www.wvmusichalloffame.com
Western Music Association. WesternMusic.org

DISCOVER THOUSANDS OF LOCAL HISTORY BOOKS
FEATURING MILLIONS OF VINTAGE IMAGES

Arcadia Publishing, the leading local history publisher in the United States, is committed to making history accessible and meaningful through publishing books that celebrate and preserve the heritage of America's people and places.

Find more books like this at
www.arcadiapublishing.com

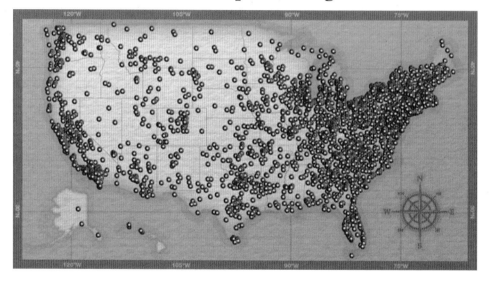

Search for your hometown history, your old stomping grounds, and even your favorite sports team.

Consistent with our mission to preserve history on a local level, this book was printed in South Carolina on American-made paper and manufactured entirely in the United States. Products carrying the accredited Forest Stewardship Council (FSC) label are printed on 100 percent FSC-certified paper.

MADE IN THE USA